The
WOMAN
ENTREPRENEUR

written and edited by:

LINDA PINSON & JERRY JINNETT

UPSTART PUBLISHING COMPANY
The Small Business Publishing Company
Dover, New Hampshire

Published by Upstart Publishing Company, Inc.
A Division of Dearborn Publishing Group, Inc.
12 Portland Street
Dover, New Hampshire 03820
(800) 235-8866 or (603) 749-5071

First published by
Out of Your Mind . . . And Into the Marketplace ™

Library of Congress Catalog Card No.: 91-090096
ISBN: 0-944205-18-6

Cover design by Indigo Graphics (Marla Jan Hauff and Pamela Simonton) and Linda Pinson and Kelley Pinson.

Printed in the United States of America
10 9 8 7 6 5 4 3 2 1

For a complete catalog of Upstart's small business publications, call (800) 235-8866.

3 9510 2001 6609 1

DEDICATION

We would like to dedicate this book to you 33 women entrepreneurs who have so generously given of your time to write your own stories so that they might serve as an inspiration to other women. You have shared your experiences and thoughts with us. We proudly present them to our readers knowing that they will be better prepared to rise to their own challenges because of your efforts.

We also dedicate the book to all future women entrepreneurs. May you have the same spirit and dedication in your ventures and emerge as successful as the women that have been profiled here.

LINDA & JERRY

ACKNOWLEDGMENT

We would like to thank all of the people who have made the production of this book go more smoothly. Lois Koehn, a long-time friend, has spent countless hours on the word-processing and coordination of material. My (Linda's) mother, Sue Area, has proof-read the book to insure that readers see fewer errors. Marla Jan Hauff and Pamela Simonton have been a great help with cover art. We would also like to thank Stacy Green who helped some of our ladies with their profiles. Last, but by no means least, a thank you goes to our families who have had the patience to live with us through the production of another book.

TABLE OF CONTENTS

PART I: HISTORY & STATISTICAL ANALYSIS 1-18
OF THE WOMAN ENTREPRENEUR

Women in History...3-5
The Women's Movement...5-6
Statistical Analysis..6-10
    Self-Employed and/or Business Owner............................6-7
    Sources of Statistics...7-8
    Comparing Data 8
        Barriers to Women Entrepreneurship...................8-9
        The National Women's Business Council...........9-10
        The Year 2000...10
    Statistical Charts...11-18
        Change in Number of Women-Owned
        Businesses by Industry (1990 Census) 12
        Change in Receipts of Women-Owned
        Businesses by Industry (1990 Census) 13
        Self-Employed Workers in Unincorporated
        Businesses by Occupation (1983 & 1990)............14-15
        Sales by Industry of U.S.
        Women-Owned Business (1990 Census).....................16
        Annual Growth by Industry,
        Men & Women Owned Businesses...........................17

PART II: 33 WOMEN ENTREPRENEURS:.......19-210
THEIR SUCCESS STORIES

   1. ENITA NORDECK
      Unity Forest Products..21-27

   2. CATHERINE ENGEL & CAROL FAGAN
      Wind Related..29-34

   3. GRACE McGARTLAND
      GM Consultants...35-39

   4. ZEE CARMAN
      New Day Enterprises, Inc. 41-45

   5. HELEN SHIH
      She's Flowers & Asian Business Connection............47-50

6. STEPHANIE SLAVIN
   Aviation Business Consultants, Inc. 51-56

7. PATTY DeDOMINIC
   PDQ Personnel Services, Inc. 57-60

8. VERA MOORE
   Vera Moore Cosmetics...61-64

9. JOANN NOONAN
   Gourmet Houston...65-69

10. CAROLINE NAKKEN & SANDRA COTTEN
    SPI - Sunshine Promotions, Inc. 71-75

11. MARTY MASCHINO
    Attic Babies...77-80

12. JOYCE McLAUGHLIN
    Interstate Tele-Marketing, Inc. 81-86

13. RUTH CHALOUS BORNAND
    Bornand Music Box Company.....................................87-91

14. O. MONA TOLIN
    Tolin Business Appraisers...93-98

15. ISOBEL B. MEDINA
    AOK Promotions...99-104

16. DAWN WELLS
    Wishing Wells Collections...105-112

17. MARIE REIKO MIYASHIRO, APR
    Marie Reiko Public Relations....................................113-118

18. GERRY VOGT
    Mrs. Gerry's Kitchen, Inc. 119-124

19. BETTYE L. SMITH
    Alaska Business College..125-131

20. JANET L. KENDRICK, M.D.
    Family Physician..133-137

21. JUDEE SLACK, EA, CFP
    Slack & Associates...139-143

22. LYNDA MILLIGAN & NANCY SMITH
    Great American Quilt Factory, Inc. 145-149

23. KATHY BRESSLER
    Cattle Kate...151-156

24. DR. JEANNE MORRIS MURRAY
    Sequoia Associates, Inc. 157-162

25. BEVERLY DURAN
    Carretas, The Cart Company....................163-166

26. LINDA WIESTER
    Cleany Boppers, Inc. 167-171

27. NORA MULHOLLAND
    The Office Furniture Broker, Inc. 173-176

28. PHYLLIS L. APELBAUM
    Arrow Messenger Service.........................177-182

29. NADIA SEMCZUK
    The Party Staff...183-187

30. ELLEN LOCKERT & NINA JACKSON
    Lockert-Jackson and Associates, Inc........189-193

31. EMILY H. MERRILL
    Brystie, Inc. 195-198

32. JACKIRAE SAGOUSPE
    International Diversified Technologies, Inc. 199-204

33. SHEILA RUDD
    Print Shop of Charleston, Inc. 205-210

PART III: RESOURCE DIRECTORY FOR STARTING YOUR BUSINESS.........211-227

How To Explore Business Ownership............................213-216
    Identifying Your Skills & Interests.......................213-215
    Develop a Business Plan..215-216
Resource Directory...217-227
    Library Resources..217-218
    U.S. Government Departments...............................219-222
    Books & Publications for the Entrepreneur........222-224
    Organizations & Associations................................224-226
    National Trade Associations..................................226-227

THE 34th PROFILE: (See the next page....)

ABOUT THE AUTHORS:

LINDA PINSON & JERRY JINNETT
Out of Your Mind...and Into the Marketplace......229-235

BUSINESS BOOKS & BUSINESS PLAN SOFTWARE AVAILABLE BY THE SAME AUTHORS 237-241

INFORMATION ON OUR SEMINARS...................................243

INTRODUCTION

One year ago, when we conceived the idea for *The Woman Entrepreneur,* we knew that it would be an interesting project. However, we had no way of understanding the possible impact it could have on our lives. We decided early on that the book would be divided into three sections...one on history and statistics, one containing profiles of successful women business owners and the third a resource section for women who might like to start their own businesses.

This seemed like a fairly simple process. The statistics could be gleaned from various reports and we would find thirty-three women and write their stories.

The statistics were there all right. However, they varied so much that it was difficult to decide which ones to use. Thus began the process of finding out how those statistics were derived and why they were so diverse. We have attempted to answer these questions in the first section of the book. It seems that there is also a time lag in the compiling of census material. Just the other day we saw a headline in a major newspaper giving the results of a comparison of revenues of men-owned versus women-owned businesses. The comparison was big news, but reflected 1987 statistics. This information is part of recently released information by the Census Bureau. For the same reason, you will find that we have included charts and graphs reflecting those time periods.

The reference section of the book was fairly straight-forward. We have listed library references, government offices, trade associations, business organizations and books and publications that might help you on the road to entrepreneurship. There are many more that would be helpful to you. They can be found through the local library, by taking classes and by talking to other business people.

The section containing the profiles proved to be the greatest surprise of all. To read well, the profiles would have to be of many different kinds of women in many different kinds of businesses. Why not have them write their own stories? It had been our experience that media features usually tell interesting stories about us, but not exactly from our own perspective. We decided that the women profiled in this book should have the chance to tell their own stories. This was an opportunity, but also meant that busy women business owners would have to take time out of their schedules to write about themselves... something that can be much more difficult than writing a complicated report.

We did have two turndowns in the process. One woman could not conceive of the concept of writing in the first person. Another was sure that "she was going to do all the work and we were going to make all the money". What she didn't realize was that writing the profiles ourselves would have been much more simple than the complications of guiding our entrepreneurs through the writing process. It was no mean task to locate thirty-three women who represented a wide variety in type of business as well as other requirements and then expect each of them to pour her heart and soul into recapping her life and her business. We owe a thank you to the SBA, NAWBO members, newspaper columnist Jan Norman and many business acquaintances for helping us to find these women and making our job easier.

The Woman Entrepreneur is mostly devoted to the profiles of those thirty-three women entrepreneurs whose success stories we have found to be both interesting and inspirational. These women all have different stories to tell, but the overriding theme is the same. Each of them has had a dream, set a goal, and been willing to work with dedication, diligence, and spirit to achieve success in her field.

It has been our privilege as authors to talk to and work with each of the women profiled. We did not interview them and write their profiles from our own viewpoint. What we asked was that each one write, in her own words, about herself and her business...and to include any advice that she would like to pass on to our readers. It might interest you to note that this was a very potent learning experience for us, as we are sure it will be for you. It is the living proof that America is truly the land of opportunity for all.

As you read ahead, you will see that our entrepreneurs represent many different ethnic groups, geographic locations, ages and types of business. Some of these women have come to the United States from other countries and have had to deal with cultural differences as well as business practices. Others have gone into male-dominated occupations and excelled in spite of closed doors. They have been willing to forge ahead to open those same doors for themselves and for future generations of women. Many are stories of successes that have risen out of the ashes of adversity, and some seem to have flowed smoothly like a river going downstream.

Almost without exception, our women entrepreneurs have expounded on the value of education and preparedness, relating both to their specific products or services and to business in general. They have voiced the need for support from family, friends, and business acquaintances. Their successes can be measured in different ways...by their volume of business, by the service they provide for others, or by the fact that they defied the odds against succeeding in their chosen fields. Many have earned our admiration because they started business as single parents and managed to forge ahead and succeed on their own. Those with spouses deserve applause, too, because in order to succeed they have had to learn the hard way how to balance their business and family lives.

As you can see, "Success" is a very subjective term. We are very proud of these thirty-three women. Each of them represents something very different in terms of what can be gleaned from her story.

All have named business as a battle, but one well worth winning. These women entered the arena and stand as victors. As such, we salute them and share their stories with you to serve as an inspiration in your own ventures.

Linda & Jerry

AWARDED BY QUALITY BOOKS, INC.

SMALL PRESS
PUBLISHER
OF THE YEAR
1989

YOUR DISTRIBUTOR TO THE LIBRARIES

The WOMAN ENTREPRENEUR

PART I

History & Statistical Analysis of the WOMAN ENTREPRENEUR

A BRIEF HISTORY
AND
CURRENT STATISTICAL ANALYSIS

It is common knowledge that women constitute more than half of this country's population (53%), but the fact that they are a growing segment of the business community is not as well known. Women-owned businesses are the fastest growing segment of small business in the nation. Before 1970, women owned 5% of all U. S. businesses. Today women own over 30% of all businesses. Women own 50% of all retail businesses and 7% of all service companies. The Bureau of the Census reports that women-owned business in the United States grew 57.5% from 1982 to 1987, from 2.162 million in 1982 to 4.614 million in 1987. Receipts grew 183% during the same time period, from $98.3 billion in 1982 to $278.1 billion in 1987.

WOMEN IN HISTORY

The emergence of women into the business arena did not occur overnight. Women through the ages have changed history by facing great personal difficulties, legal barriers, ridicule and danger to pursue their dreams of entrepreneurship and business ownership. The efforts of early women entrepreneurs were hampered by laws which prevented them from entering into contracts, owning property, or bringing legal suits. Husbands could prevent their wives from opening bank accounts or starting businesses. A husband could claim all of a wife's wages in order to settle his debts. A single woman was allowed to retain sole ownership of property, draft legal documents and have access to the courts through a deputy. However, she did not have the right to be named as a beneficiary in her father's will. The following entrepreneurs are representative of the women who persevered and succeeded in business and formed the foundation of success for other women:

MADAME VEUVE CLIQUOT

In an age when commerce was considered socially improper for a woman, Madame Veuve Cliquot (1770-1866) assumed control of her family's champagne house as a young widow. Her innovative techniques revolutionized the industry and she guided the company to a position of international excellence. The House of Veuve Cliquot continues to reign as one of the most distinguished and successful of all the great Champagne Houses.

SARAH BUELL HALE

Sarah Buell Hale (1788-1879) taught school until her marriage in 1813. Her husband died in 1822 and she found herself the sole support of her 5 children. She began writing and became editor of the Boston Ladies' Magazine. During her career, she exerted a nation-wide influence. She encouraged women writers, working tirelessly for the cause of higher education for women.

REBECCA WEBB LUKENS

When Rebecca Webb Lukens (1794-1854) assumed control of the financially ailing Brandywine Mill in Coalesville, Pennsylvania upon her husband's death, she became the first woman in America to enter the iron industry. Under her leadership, the mill regained financial stability and became a very strong and widely respected business. The Brandywine Iron Works was renamed the Lukens Iron Works upon her death.

VICTORIA WOODHULL

Victoria Woodhull (1832-1927) and her sister, Tennessee Claflin, founded the first stockbrokerage firm owned by women. She published a periodical endorsing women's rights to suffrage, to financial independence, and to birth control. She became the first woman to run for the presidency in 1872 on the Equal Rights Ticket.

REBECCA KNOX

After the death of her husband, Rebecca Knox (1857-1950), co-founder of Knox Gelatin, Inc., took full control and led the company into successful expansion. The Knox company became the leading manufacturer and distributor of gelatin. She was named the first woman director of the American Grocery Manufacturers Association and was President and Chairman of the Board of Knox Gelatin until her death.

THE WOMEN'S MOVEMENT

In the 1940's the American economy and work force were changed forever. As men were called into the armed forces during The Second World War, women replaced them in the work force. The defense industry opened additional job opportunities for women. They began developing the skills and confidence needed to compete in business.

The Women's Movement sparked significant social and economic changes in the 1970's. According to the U. S. Department of Labor, the number of nonfarm sole proprietorships operated by women increased from 1.9 million in 1977 to 3.3 million in 1983, an annual growth rate of 9.4 percent.

Women-owned businesses have traditionally been concentrated in the services and in the retail trade industries. In the past, most companies started by women specialized in food, fashion, or other areas which have been traditionally viewed as "women's work". A five-year survey entitled "1987 Women-Owned Businesses" was released in October of 1990 by the

United States Census Bureau and showed that the movement into nontraditional fields was dramatic.

Women-owned construction businesses showed a fourfold increase in receipts from 1982 to 1987, while women-owned manufacturing companies earned nearly six times more than they had five years before. In the wholesale trade industry, the number of women-owned firms rose from 30,059 to 82,513 for an increase of more than 157%. The SBA predicts that women-owned businesses will continue to be the fastest-growing sector in the U. S. economy.

As women business owners expand their companies, they will add substantially to the economic growth of the local, regional, and national economies. For example between 1982 and 1987, the number of women-owned firms with paid employees nearly doubled, providing a wealth of needed jobs to more than 3 million American workers. In the same time frame, women-owned businesses' total receipts nearly tripled previous figures, from about $98 billion to $278 billion, accounting for 14 percent of the nation's business receipts.

STATISTICAL ANALYSIS

SELF-EMPLOYED AND/OR BUSINESS OWNER?

In reviewing statistics on women entrepreneurs, it is important to understand that there is some overlap between the terms "self-employed" and "business owner." The fundamental distinction between the two concerns the context in which they are used. Self-employment is a concept used in household surveys to describe a person's labor market status. In principal, all full-time business owners who derive most of their income from their businesses can be considered self-employed. However, statistics published by the Bureau of Labor Statistics (BLS) on self-employment do not include incorporated self-employed individuals, that is, those business owners whose businesses are organized as corporations. They are considered to be employees of their businesses. The Internal Revenue Service (IRS) on the other hand, includes full-time and part-time, incorporated and unincorporated business owners in its data. The number of nonfarm sole proprietorships reported by the IRS will therefore be higher than the number of self-employed individuals reported by BLS.

WOMAN-OWNED BUSINESS

The Census Bureau classifies a business as woman-owned if 50% or more of the business' owners are women. For example, if four of the eight owners of a partnership are women, the Census Bureau would classify the partnership as women-owned. Subchapter S corporations where 50 percent or more of the shareholders are women are classified as women-owned. From the IRS's Statistics of Income sample of proprietors, a determination of business ownership is made by the IRS on the basis of the name listed on the Schedule C tax form. The business is then classified as man-owned, woman-owned, or jointly owned. The Census definition of women-owned businesses as those 50 percent or more owned by women presents a problem in assigning gender to those businesses owned by both husband and wife. When records indicate that both spouses own a business the Census Bureau assumes owners to be equal and recognizes equal ownership as women's ownership. This creates comparability problems with IRS data and results in an overcount of businesses owned by women.

SOURCES OF STATISTICS

The most comprehensive source of federal statistics on women-owned businesses are collected and disseminated under the Survey of Women-Owned Business (WOB), a special program of the Census Bureau's Economic Censuses. The most recent WOB data (1987) revealed that there were approximately 4.1 million businesses owned by women, with combined receipts of $278.1 billion. These data reveal an increase of about 58 percent since 1982 in the number of women-owned businesses covered by the Census survey.

According to the National Survey of Small Business Finances (NSSBF), there were 184,103 regular corporations owned by women in 1987, with total receipts of approximately $198.8 billion.

COMPARING DATA

The combined WOB and NSSBF data reveal that in 1987 there were approximately 4.3 million women-owned businesses with total receipts of $476.9 billion.

These estimates, when compared with the Census Bureau and Internal Revenue Service estimates for the total U.S. business population, establish an approximate lower boundary for the share of women-owned businesses and business receipts. These totals indicate that about 26.6% of U.S. businesses are owned by women and that these businesses account for approximately 4.5% of total U. S. business receipts.

Megatrends 2000 forecasts that one of the most important trends influencing our lives in the 1990's is the "Decade of Women in Leadership: the Decade of Women in Business." Women-owned businesses have attained an important place alongside businesses owned by men. The growth rate of women-owned businesses, both in number and average receipts, continues to exceed that for businesses owned by men. The 1987 Census reports that women start businesses at a rate twice as fast as men. Moreover, women can be expected to continue their progress into the labor force and business ownership. Their determination and increasing industrial diversification represent important steps toward economic and personal fulfillment as well as economic growth and strength for the nation.

BARRIERS TO WOMEN ENTREPRENEURSHIP

In 1979, Charlotte Taylor prepared a Presidential Report entitled "The Bottom Line: Unequal Enterprise in America". The report indicated that women business owners experience the following barriers to entrepreneurship:

1. Limited access to commercial credit.

2. Virtual exclusion of women-owned business from government procurement activities.

3. Limited management and technical training to "fast-track" women into the marketplace.

4. Inadequate information and data on women-owned business.

Ten years later, in 1988, the same barriers were identified during congressional hearings held to explore the economic growth and impact of women business owners. These hearings, conducted by Representative John LaFalce, Chairman of the Committee on Small Business, determined that not much change had taken place since Charlotte Taylor conducted her study in 1979. The House Small Business Committee hearings found that women business owners still faced considerable difficulties, especially in bidding on government contracts and in gaining access to commercial credit.

The availability of capital is of primary concern both in starting a new business and in expanding. According to a recent study conducted for the SBA, individual savings are the major source of equity capital for women and joint savings of husband and wife rank second. Other sources are friends and relatives, other individuals, and various financial institutions. The majority of companies currently owned by women were started with less than $5,000. Many banks will not extend commercial loans to women unless their husbands or other men in the family co-sign the application.

THE NATIONAL WOMEN'S BUSINESS COUNCIL

At the end of these hearings a report entitled "New Economic Realities, the Rise of Women Entrepreneurs" was issued. One of the most significant recommendations of the report resulted in the formation of the National Women's Business Council. The NWBC is charged with developing recommendations which establish a national policy supporting women entrepreneurs. The NWBC has proposed a Women's Economic Summit to be held in May, 1992 for the purpose of analyzing the history of women in business, reviewing the present, and planning for the future.

THE YEAR 2000

By the year 2000, women will make up 59% of the labor force. According to the National Association of Women Business Owners (NAWBO), 84% of them will be employed in the service and information sectors and 51% will be employed by small businesses. Women will also be realizing their dreams of business ownership. In 1990, over 39% of small businesses (not including full corporations) were owned by women, and the Small Business Administration projects that women will own 50% of the small businesses in America in the 21st century. In no other country have women undertaken business ownership in such large numbers.

The world has entered an era of unparalleled demographic, political, and economic change. Women entrepreneurs are already a major contributing force and are becoming even more so as we move toward the next century.

———————————————

CHARTS & GRAPHS .

The next six pages of this book contain statistical information in the form of charts and graphs. Many of them show changes in data relating to women-owned businesses for the years from 1982 through 1987.

The 1987 Census Bureau Report was not released until September of 1990. There is about a three-year time lag between the gathering of information and its release.

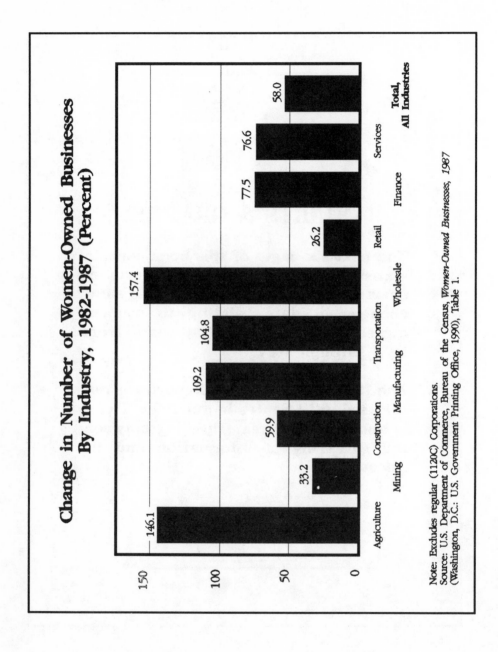

Change in Number of Women-Owned Businesses By Industry, 1982-1987 (Percent)

Agriculture: 146.1
Mining: 33.2
Construction: 59.9
Manufacturing: 109.2
Transportation: 104.8
Wholesale: 157.4
Retail: 26.2
Finance: 77.5
Services: 76.6
Total, All Industries: 58.0

Note: Excludes regular (1120C) Corporations.
Source: U.S. Department of Commerce, Bureau of the Census, *Women-Owned Businesses, 1987* (Washington, D.C.: U.S. Government Printing Office, 1990), Table 1.

12

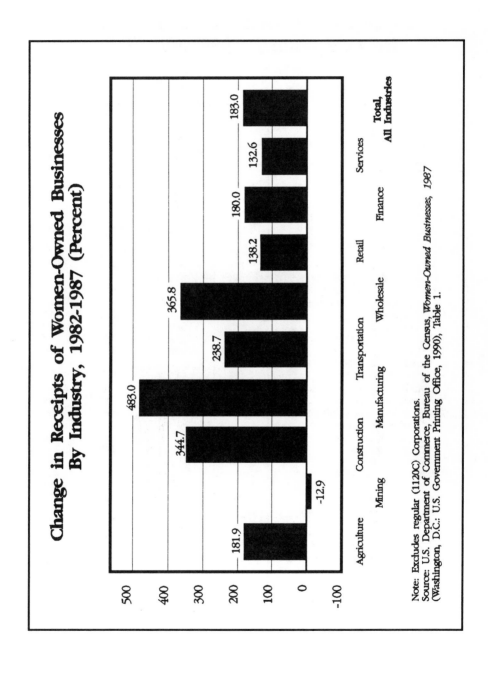

**Change in Receipts of Women-Owned Businesses
By Industry, 1982-1987 (Percent)**

Industry	Percent
Agriculture	181.9
Mining	-12.9
Construction	344.7
Manufacturing	483.0
Transportation	238.7
Wholesale	365.8
Retail	138.2
Finance	180.0
Services	132.6
Total, All Industries	183.0

Note: Excludes regular (1120C) Corporations.
Source: U.S. Department of Commerce, Bureau of the Census, *Women-Owned Businesses, 1987* (Washington, D.C.: U.S. Government Printing Office, 1990), Table 1.

13

SELF-EMPLOYED WORKERS
IN UNINCORPORATED BUSINESSES
by Occupation, 1983 and 1990

Note: Numbers in Thousands

OCCUPATION	1983		1990	
	Total	Percent Women	Total	Percent Women
Total, all occupations.........	9,101	29.0	10,133	33.1
Executive, administrative, and managerial occupations.	1,212	23.3	1,606	26.1
Managers, properties and real estate.	87	33.6	90	27.7
Accountants and auditors.	103	19.7	105	28.2
Management analysts	43	20.5	68	28.3
Professional specialty occupations. .	1,234	32.0	1,467	35.2
Health diagnosing occupations. .	264	6.8	297	12.2
Physicians	133	10.1	136	14.7
Dentists	80	2.9	92	7.1
Teachers except postsecondary	139	77.8	133	71.4
Lawyers	209	10.6	196	13.6
Writers, artists, entertainers, and athletes	413	44.5	517	47.8
Authors	50	46.3	63	60.7
Designers	91	69.4	115	66.9
Musicians and composers . . .	70	17.7	76	18.2
Painters, sculptors, craft-artists, and artist printmakers	99	54.6	116	54.6
Photographers	42	19.3	49	24.5
Technicians and related support occupations	57	32.5	82	31.9
Sales occupations	1,769	37.6	1,820	37.2
Supervisors and proprietors, sales occupations	752	30.9	768	35.1
Sales representatives, finance and business services. . .	520	24.7	631	28.2
Insurance sales occupations	116	12.1	138	17.0
Real estate sales occupations	197	41.1	248	45.6
Sales workers, retail and personal services	483	61.6	406	55.1
Street and door-to-door sales workers	211	87.8	145	81.0
Administrative support occupations including clerical	246	82.3	329	83.7

Source: *Occupational Outlook Quarterly*, Spring 1991
NOTE: Detail may not add to totals due to rounding.

SELF-EMPLOYED WORKERS
IN UNINCORPORATED BUSINESSES
by Occupation, 1983 and 1990

Note: Numbers in Thousands

OCCUPATION	1983		1990	
	Total	Percent Women	Total	Percent Women
Self-Employed Workers Table page no. 2				
Secretaries, stenographers, and typists.	61	90.5	86	96.0
Bookkeepers and accounting and auditing clerks	121	87.2	139	91.1
Service occupations	889	77.7	1,211	82.2
Protective service occupations	9	6.9	7	9.5
Food preparation and service occupations.	97	49.8	73	51.9
Cleaning and building service occupations except private household	98	45.5	224	68.8
Personal service occupations. . .	673	87.1	873	88.3
Hairdressers and cosmetologists	249	90.1	297	88.7
Child care workers except private household	345	99.5	475	98.9
Farming, forestry, and fishing occupations.	1,572	12.5	1,377	14.9
Farm operators and managers . .	1,313	12.5	1,076	15.4
Precision production, craft, and repair occupations.	1,543	7.4	1,677	7.3
Mechanics and repairers	421	0.8	413	1.9
Construction trades	887	2.2	1,054	2.8
Carpenters	327	1.0	373	1.0
Painters, construction and maintenance	156	4.7	193	7.3
Plumbers, pipefitters, and steamfitters	54	1.1	66	1.1
Operators, fabricators, and laborers.	579	13.6	563	19.7
Motor vehicle operators.	289	5.1	247	6.3
Truck drivers, heavy	209	2.7	152	2.5
Taxicab drivers and chauffeurs	39	6.3	48	5.7

Source: *Occupational Outlook Quarterly*, Spring 1991

NOTE: Detail may not add to totals due to rounding.

SALES (PERCENT) BY INDUSTRY
U.S. WOMEN-OWNED BUSINESS

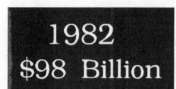

1982
$98 Billion

■ Retail

▫ Transportation

▤ Manufacturing

▨ Construction

■ Finance

▦ Agric., Other

▨ Wholesale

□ Services

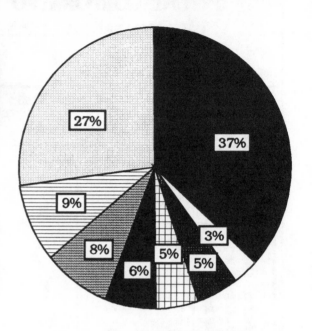

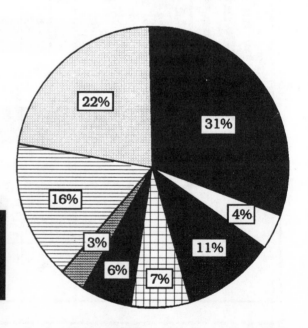

1987
$278 Billion

Compiled by the U.S. Department of Commerce, Economic Censuses, 1990

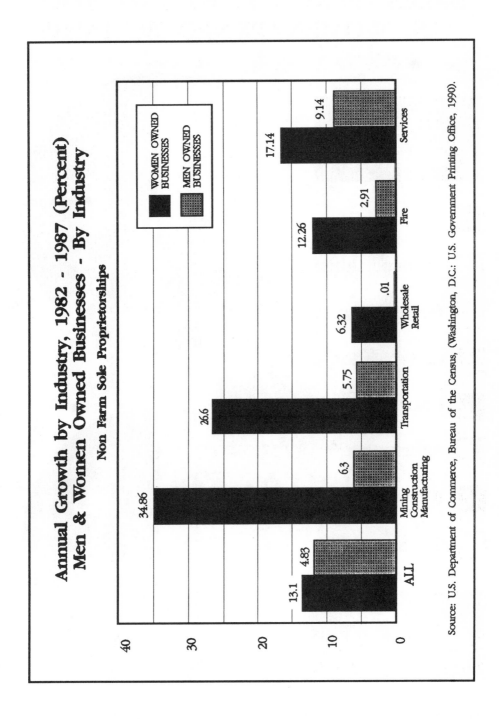

**Annual Growth by Industry, 1982 - 1987 (Percent)
Men & Women Owned Businesses - By Industry**

Non Farm Sole Proprietorships

WOMEN OWNED BUSINESSES

MEN OWNED BUSINESSES

ALL: 13.1 / 4.83

Mining Construction Manufacturing: 34.86 / 6.3

Transportation: 26.6 / 5.75

Wholesale Retail: 6.32 / .01

Fire: 12.26 / 2.91

Services: 17.14 / 9.14

Source: U.S. Department of Commerce, Bureau of the Census, (Washington, D.C.: U.S. Government Printing Office, 1990).

The WOMAN ENTREPRENEUR

PART II

33 Women Entrepreneurs

THEIR SUCCESS STORIES

ENITA NORDECK

UNITY FOREST PRODUCTS

Enita Nordeck is the President, owner, and founder of Unity Forest Products, a multimillion dollar lumber remanufacturing company located in Yuba City, California. Throughout her life she has broken barriers for women. She is the only known woman to build and manage a lumber mill; the first woman to be elected trustee of the local unified school board. She is the first woman and first lumber industry leader to receive the U.S. Small Business Administration Northern California "Small Business Person of the Year" Award (1991), and the first person in the lumber industry to receive the Girl Scout Role Model of the Year Award (1991). Enita Nordeck inspires people whose lives she touches, men and women alike. She personifies the success achieved through determination - determination to overcome a lack of formal education, poverty, divorce, and raising a family alone.

21

"It wasn't until later in the lumber business that I became aware of the fact that a woman shouldn't have been able to do this in a man's world.....

When I was a young girl growing up on top of California's Sonoma mountains, I never envisioned having the ability or the means to own my own business. Certainly not a fifteen million dollar-a-year lumber mill. My visions were filled with science labs, test tubes holding exciting chemicals, and blackboards filled with magical formulas and complex mathematical equations.

But reality was older parents and a dying ranch incapable of providing the simplest necessities. At the age of 66, my father lost everything: the ranch, our home and even the furniture. What the bank left behind was taken by creditors. This experience would have broken most people, but not my father.

I've never been a person who had to learn from actual experience; observation has always been sufficient. And what I observed over the following years proved invaluable in my future endeavors. From my parents I learned to address adversity with determination and hard work. I watched my father, then 66, begin work as a laborer for a dairy ranch to support his wife and two small children. This enabled him to put mother, then in her fifties, through college. Mother finished four years of college in two years and started working with a provisional teaching degree. Dad's health had failed from the long, hard hours of labor. Mother also was exhausted, studying incessantly for two years. But they obtained their goal, a means of supporting their family.

By the time I reached high school, observation proved that hard work and determination weren't the only ingredients in the formula for success. Knowledge and the application of that knowledge was necessary. I discovered that knowledge was infinite and powerful. Had my youngest brother and I been just a little older during my parents' struggle on the ranch, it could have been saved. The missing ingredient had been knowledge, the basic competence in current day business management. With this observation I pursued my quest for knowledge with a vengeance. Aware that college was probably an unobtainable goal, I still took every college-prep class available. My goal was not to earn straight A's in school, but to gather and retain knowledge. It was during this period that a poem crossed my path which had a tremendous impact on me. It put into precise words the feelings I had absorbed during my childhood.

> "Let us be up and doing
> With a heart for any faith
> Still achieving - still pursuing
> Learn to labor and to wait."

As Valedictorian of my high school class and winner of myriad awards, several universities approached me about attending their campuses. But this was not to be. My parents' financial position was still tenuous and both were very ill. Their fear of my being alone without their protection moved them to ask me not to attend college, but to marry and stay close. To them marriage was the only safe haven for a single young woman. Their reasons for asking me to stay were based on fear for my well-being. To this day I am thankful I stayed.

Within a month of high school graduation, I had married and obtained a file clerk job at the local sawmill. Thus began my career in the lumber industry. The following years were filled with ever-expanding goals. First were the basics of earning a living, helping my parents, making my husband happy, and just surviving. Two years after my marriage and two children later, added was the goal of being a good parent. By the time my third child was born two years later, I had progressed in my career, focusing my ambitions on the office manager position. My father passed away during this period with my mother following shortly thereafter.

During this whole process I learned it wasn't enough to simply 'do' the job. The pursuit of knowledge was never-ending. And I was lucky. The men working at the sawmill were intelligent, hard-working, and most were more than willing to impart their knowledge. I have found this to be true throughout my career. But you must seek knowledge, not stand passively by and expect it to be handed to you.

My children's education was of supreme importance to me. After finding that one of my children had a learning disability, I ran for the Unified School Board of Trustees. By the time my fourth child arrived, I had been President of the Board of Trustees for four years and obtained the office manager position at the sawmill. But more important than any title, I had learned the lumber business, from building roads to harvesting timber, and all the facets of lumber manufacturing.

It wasn't until later, and someone else pointed it out, that I became aware a woman shouldn't have been able to do this in a man's world. It never seemed strange being the only woman at meetings or on the sawmill floor. I respected the men for their knowledge and abilities and they respected me for mine. It was never a question of being a woman in a male-dominated field; it was a question of knowledge. There are reams of articles printed regarding women and the inequities they face in the work arena. Fortunately, I was blessed with an ignorance of this fact. Never have I desired to be equal to a man. We are different and thank God for that difference. But being different does not mean one is less than the other - to the contrary - women have the ability to far exceed men in some areas, and not just on the home front but also in the work arena. We perceive and apply information differently.

A good example is motivation. Men tend to expect people to be self-motivated, while women tend to motivate people. This motivational skill, if applied, is invaluable in business. Maybe the average woman can't lift 150 pounds with the ease of the average man, but most women wouldn't want to. However, we do have the ability to motivate and direct the lifting of thousands of pounds safely and efficiently. Women, as do men, tend to create their own problems by being dishonest with themselves. We say we want equality and yet, I have observed over the years that many of us aren't willing to pay the price for the so-called 'equality'. We want to excel in our work area and yet complain that it leaves no time to be a mother, no time to be ourselves. This is dishonest. Of course we can be mothers, homemakers and still excel in our professions. But the price is self-determination, hard work, and responsibility to our family, to our employer, and to ourselves.

After 17 years of marriage, 17 years of working, and four children, ages sixteen, fifteen, thirteen, and four, I took time to evaluate where I was and where I wanted to go. And thus started some of the most painful and, ultimately, most rewarding years of my life. There were vital differences between my goals and those of my husband. I wanted to be up and doing, still pursuing. He was content where we were. I felt I had labored and waited long enough and any longer would be too late. At age 35, I would be over fifty before all my children were raised. So with extreme fear and a deep sense of guilt, I left my husband, took the four children, and started again. According to the experts' books, I did everything wrong. But once again I was blessed with ignorance of this fact. I moved, took the children, and accepted a job I knew nothing about (Controller for a lumber manufacturing plant). I refused alimony and child support, divided all the assets, and took all the liabilities. This was my decision; therefore my responsibility.

Divorce can be very destructive if we allow it. It is easy to tear down, tear apart. The real challenge is to maintain a respect for the other parent, and allow your children the pride and dignity of both parents. I found myself working along parallel tracks, laboring with equal zeal on my children's emotional, educational, and physical needs; while striving toward my own professional goals. The fear of being unable to maintain the pace necessary to protect my family was sometimes overwhelming. Objective evaluation would always affirm my choice, I had to press on.

At the end of those first seven years alone, I had developed the ability to turn financially unstable sawmills and lumber remanufacturing companies into profitable businesses. I was on two boards of directorship, chief financial officer for three companies, and general manager of a lumber remanufacturing plant. And finally, I was financially secure and my children were becoming responsible, productive, loving people.

I remarried, but this time it was my decision. He was a person so secure in himself and his worth that my goals did not frighten or challenge him. For once I had several options and again paused to evaluate where I was and where I wanted to go. After this appraisal, I decided to do something different. What? I didn't know. But with my husband's blessings, I resigned from all my professional commitments.

And so the next chapter of my life began. A few weeks after I had left my employment, three gentlemen who had worked for me (the best in their chosen fields) appeared on my door step. They looked at me and stated forcibly, 'We've quit our jobs. We know you'll do something and whatever it is, we want to do it with you. And we're going to sit here on your door step until you do.' I'll never forget that moment. I looked at them and the wheels started turning. I left the door open, turned around, walked into the living room where my husband was reading the paper. As I approached him, ideas were forming in my mind. By the time I reached his chair I'd decided what I wanted to do. I remember asking, 'Honey, do you mind if I start my own lumber business?' He answered, 'No'. My response was laced with fear, 'But it'll take everything we have and possibly, if I fail, everything we will ever have.' Again his answer was short, 'I have faith in you.' But still I persisted, 'If I do this, you won't really see me for a year - it'll take that long to get it on its feet.' Once again he looked up at me, 'Are you sure you can do it in that time frame?' My answer was a quick, unequivocal 'Yes'. And his response was just as quick, 'Then do it.' So I went back to the front door and addressed the three young men still standing on my porch. 'O.K. gentlemen, won't you come in - here's what we're going to do...'

Within the first week, I had sold my house and started liquidating my assets. UFP started business just two weeks after the idea was conceived; without benefit of financing, office, phones, pencils, or even a stapler. The following year was filled with the most intense application of knowledge I have every experienced. When faced with closed doors, we opened them. The banks repeatedly said 'No' to financing a start-up company. Yet with a detailed five-year business plan in hand (one I revised many times), I refused to accept 'No'. With this determination, not only was a bank convinced to provide the necessary financing, but also the State of California and the City of Yuba City, under a Federal Loan Program. When no suitable manufacturing facility could be found, we decided to build one.

The impossible was not only accomplished, but accomplished on schedule and within budget. In that first year we grossed 6 million dollars, booked a healthy profit and built a million-dollar facility. The second year we grossed 10 million; the third year 15 million. This year we'll break our record again. UFP's accomplishments are the direct result of applied knowledge and motivated, loyal people. The three young men who stood on my doorstep that day never faltered. Shortly after forming UFP, several highly skilled men (men whose skills I needed desperately) approached me wanting to work for me. I explained we couldn't pay what their current employers were paying, nor even promise UFP would survive the first year. Each of their answers was simple: 'I have faith in you--you'll make it work. The pay doesn't matter. I want to work for you.'

How can a company fail with that kind of motivation and loyalty; that willingness to 'labor and wait'? And although childhood visions and magical formulas, complex mathematical equations and science labs may never have materialized, no child could envision the rewards reaped from constantly pursuing and incessant 'laboring and waiting'."

UNITY FOREST PRODUCTS
P. O. Box 1849, Yuba City, CA 95992
TEL: (916) 671-7152, (800) 248-4940, FAX: (916) 671-7357

CATHERINE ENGEL & CAROL FAGAN

WIND RELATED

Sisters Catherine Engel (left) and Carol Fagan (right) of Hamilton, Montana merged their talents in biology and sewing to translate biological forms into three-dimensional wind art. Wind Related began as a family project. Manufacturing was done in their parents' basement. Catherine drove 30,000 miles in 4 months to establish accounts while the family stayed home and filled orders. Catherine and Carol were chosen as Montana Small Business Persons of the Year 1990 and Wind Related has successfully grown from a home-based business to one that is national in scope, but still personal in nature.

Catherine and Carol were both born in California. Catherine attended U.C., San Diego and Santa Barbara, was a recipient of a Fulbright-Hays Scholarship in 1970 and received her Ph.D. in Zoology in 1976. Catherine has worked in various media including batik, fabric painting and gyotaku and has exhibited in solo and group shows, including a Smithsonian S.I.T.E.S., touring the United States, Australia, China and Japan. Carol attended the School of Life with Masters in Child Rearing, Housekeeping and Wifery. She has worked 18 years manufacturing clothing and specialty outdoor products with an emphasis on custom design. Her artistic talents cover several years of airbrushed, one of a kind clothing, hang glider sails and paintings.

29

"Greetings from the Big Sky Country of Montana - home of blue skies and unlimited opportunities for those willing to work for their dreams.....

I am Catherine Engel and with my sister, Carol Fagan, the dream of Wind Related blossomed into a business in a small town in the Bitterroot Valley of Montana in 1985. I had spoken to Carol about my idea of making three-dimensional windsocks, patterned after native wildflower species. Carol's husband was terminally ill and she realized she needed to support her family. Carol considered her background in business and commercial sewing and proposed to me that we merge our talents and go into business together using my windsock idea.

With my Ph.D. in Zoology and experience as a biologist and Carol's experience in manufacturing and sewing, we drew up a business plan for Wind Works - our initial company name. We had an innovative, exciting concept utilizing a special lightweight ripstop nylon in bright colors to give a glowing effect to the windsocks in sunlight. We could not find any financing - banks felt our business wouldn't 'fly' and the SBA turned us down because the loan amount requested didn't meet their minimum. It was very frustrating. We were operating in a 'boy's club' mentality that looked upon women entrepreneurs as small time operators that would never enter the real business world. We had no assets and no capital, just a strong desire to succeed and see our business grow. Our grandmother, Clarice Pierson, offered us a $20,000 line of credit secured by a C.D., to be repaid with interest. This got the ball rolling and we implemented our business plan.

The designing process was a challenge in translating biological forms into three-dimensional wind art. This work has really increased my awareness of the various ways to see forms and textures in nature. In the design process I try to capture the correct botanical or biological form with key characters, colors and shapes. In addition I prepare detailed educational inserts for each design. These inserts also draw upon my background in biology and besides being very informative they provide an interesting extra added attraction to the end product. Plus, they were a vehicle to establish us in the non-profit market of museum gift shops. We were on the forefront of educational packaging for museum status. This enabled us to create a strong museum gift shop base.

With fifteen years experience in manufacturing products for outdoor equipment, Carol took on the manufacturing portion of Wind Related. We started out in her kitchen and then moved to our parents' basement. Here we set up a production facility complete with all the cutting, finishing and shipping processes. Our father, Earl Pollard, handled the cutting, Carol's son, Jonathan, did the finishing and our mother, Eileen, helped in shipping. Carol continued to work on all these aspects as well as sew at home. At that time we started contracting out as much sewing as possible to home based independent contractors. These are primarily housewives and mothers who choose the flexibility of being in business for themselves.

I had no business background and starting a sales and marketing program was a real learning process. I designed twelve wildflower Windflowers and targeted national park, museum and airport gift shops. Carol took my designs and adapted the pattern pieces to commercial sewing methods. We designed our business cards, stationary, order forms and headers for our packaging. We hired a professional local photographer to take photos for our brochure; however, the results were dismal. Windsocks are difficult to photograph in the outdoors and I decided to work on my own photographic efforts. I discovered a technique that worked well and I've done all the photography.

Next we had to establish some accounts, so I got in my car and hit the road with twelve samples and a display stand developed by our father. I drove over 30,000 miles in the next four months throughout the western states, and I developed a good case of carpel tunnel in my arms for my efforts from the vibration of the steering wheel and carrying a giant bag with my samples and the stand. I would drive into a town, cruise the streets and note shops that looked promising and then hit a telephone booth and make appointments. I didn't know any sales techniques - I just figured if you told someone you were coming they were obliged to listen to you. A common response was 'What good is it?' or my favorite 'Is this a new type of hosiery?' I tried to convey my enthusiasm to the buyer and once they saw the windsocks I often got orders. Since this was a new concept, I also had to go into detail on how to display and sell my product - mostly common sense on my part since I was new to the marketing scene. But it worked! I would phone orders home and the family would ship them out.

By the end of the summer we had established over 200 accounts and discovered trade shows. They were fantastic - people came to me and actually asked to order. I was in heaven! This was the turning point for our business because along with reaching a national market came networking with other crafts people who were seeking to enter the wholesale gift market as small manufacturers of handcrafted items. In talking to fellow exhibitors I found out about other trade shows, publications to advertise in and the ins-and-outs of credit. I cannot emphasize enough how important networking was to the growth and success of our business.

As Carol explains, there are two major production factors which have been key contributors to the success of our business. One is production methods and the other is our employees. We have been innovative in utilizing manufacturing techniques from other industries and adapting them for our uses. We simply won't accept the 'usual' method as the only method, but always keep an open mind and look for a better way. Emphasis on cross-training results in greater efficiency and improves employee morale with increased responsibilities within the manufacturing process.

Wind Related prides itself on offering a quality product and excellent service and the employees' concern for quality is a major contributor to the success of the business. We encourage our employees to use creative thinking in relation to their jobs. When they come up with an idea, we listen, we consider, and in many cases implement their ideas. We work together as a team towards common goals. We maintain a positive attitide and offer praise and appreciation for a job well done. Each week

32

everyone participates in the 'Personnel Best Hour,' a self-enrichment program that includes both the practical such as CPR training and stress management as well as sharing personal interests, including needlepoint techniques or good recipes.

Production methods and employees are key cogs in manufacturing. It is the marketing efforts that keep the gears moving. In order to succeed you must set goals, have a sound business plan and good management for implementation. We have constantly set new goals and revised our business plan.

In 1986, we ran into a problem with our business name and I bring this up because it is important for a start up business. If you plan to sell outside your state (think big!) check with the National Register to make sure you are not infringing upon someone else's registered or trademark name. If you receive a letter claiming you are infringing, follow-up and check to see that this is indeed the case. Another Wind Works asked us to quit using 'their name' and having to change cost us a great deal of time and money. At first we couldn't think of another name, and then we decided that whatever we were going to be doing it would be 'wind related.' Ah ha, that was it!

In our first year of business we exhibited in eleven trade shows and advertised in five national trade publications. We also had our first four-color brochure printed which greatly improved our national marketing efforts. Advertising agencies were expensive, so all our advertising was done in-house, from line drawings and ad format to brochure design and photography. I did get the type set which made our advertising much more professional looking than my initial typewritten efforts. We made a point of doing new ads every month presenting new items or lines. That strategy helped increase our market base at a rapid pace.

Another strategy that increased our national market was to hire sales reps. However, initially our pricing did not take into account the sales reps percentage (15% for our industry). Pricing is critical to the success of a business and I encourage anyone going into manufacturing to seek professional help in pricing (the local SBA will offer assistance). Today we know the exact cost of every item we manufacture and we work a sales rep percentage into the pricing.

From the beginning we have marketed heavily to mail order catalogs. You must plan 6 months to 2 years in advance for catalog sales, however the effort is well worth the returns. This has been one other key to our success - we have an incredibly wide base - from gift shops, florists, museums, hardware stores, botanical gardens, aquariums, kite stores, marinas, art galleries - you name it. And by expanding our product lines we are moving into new areas such as hospitals, retail display, cemeteries, and stationary stores.

Whenever possible we send out media kits and solicit free advertising with articles in magazines, newspapers and journals. And then there are the 'out of the blue' photos or articles that appear - such as the photo of actress Glenn Close with our macaw windsock hanging over her head like a hat. That appeared in a popular national monthly and gave us valuable exposure. Being chosen as the Small Business Persons of the Year in Montana in 1990 was very exciting for us and it brought us a lot of congratulations and new accounts. We were especially amazed at the number of insurance agents who suddenly discovered us and wanted our business. It was gratifying to be recognized in our local area and now be accepted as a part of what used to be a male domain.

Wind Related is dedicated to producing a handcrafted, quality product that is both beautiful and educational. Wind Related will continue to expand the limits of wind art, as well as entering new spheres of exploration such as office supplies and clothing. We started as a home based business, we are now national in scope but Wind Related is still a small, personal business and we intend to stay that way."

WIND RELATED, INC.
1595 N. First Street, Hamilton, MT 59840
TEL: (406) 363-1050

GRACE McGARTLAND

GM CONSULTANTS

Grace McGartland founded GM Consultants in 1981 and it has expanded into a successful consulting firm serving clients nationally and internationally. Grace uses her expertise in the areas of planning, creative thinking and training through presentations and speeches. Struck by cancer in 1984, this dynamic lady faced her greatest challenge and emerged with new insight and a new set of goals. In addition to expanding her own business, Grace has become a national leader in the women's business arena. She is currently serving as President-elect on the National Board of Directors for NAWBO and previously served as vice president of membership, vice president of marketing and co-chair of NAWBO's National Marketing Task Force. Grace is Director of the National Foundation for Women Business Owners. In Pittsburgh, she was a chairperson of the Women's Entrepreneurial Partnership and was president of Pittsburgh Volunteers for Appalachian Health for 13 years. Recent awards include NAWBO's 1989-90 National President's Award; the Small Business Administration's 1989 regional Women in Business Advocate Award; Norman Link Memorial Award.

"The real challenge was not dealing with death but creating a life worth living.....

August 1981. This was the beginning of the 1981 recession, and I had not a shred of business experience. Starting a new business now was not what most people would call a logical step, but my vision was strong. I felt ready to combine my master's degree in Communications and Technology with my eight years of experience as an educator and begin developing communication tools for business. I imagined myself as a 'schoolmarm' with a twist, helping my 'students' (clients) to free their thinking and develop successful strategic and marketing plans. Late nights during graduate school when my thoughts wandered to the future, I saw myself sketching designs...speaking to groups...on the phone with clients, bankers, and accountants...in other words, being an entrepreneur.

What keeps my vision strong is a creative strategy called Estimated Time of Arrival (ETA). ETA asks you to picture-envision your arrival at your goal. When you can almost reach out and touch success, it makes it easier to make it happen. Your priorities become easier to set. When I daydreamed about being a successful entrepreneur, I was helping myself to make it happen. ETA also helped me keep GM Consultants going despite the upheaval of my divorce, coming just 18 months after I'd started my company.

Ten years later, my company has metamorphosed into an international consulting firm, with expertise in strategic planning, strategic marketing, and strategy-thinking processes. As our clients have grown and changed, we've enhanced our services to meet their needs. Consequently, GM Consultants developed a unique and effective mode, THUNDERBOLT TRANSFORMATION, that blends people and the environment in a catalytic process that takes advantage of brainpower as a strategic weapon to meet business goals. This process, Displayed Thinking, invented by Leonardo da Vinci, helps senior decision-makers transform their organizations by smashing thinking gridlocks, breaking traditional mindsets, and reshaping thinking patterns to define steps for action and get bottom-line business results.

What actually propelled THUNDERBOLT TRANSFORMATION was the biggest challenge that I've encountered, and it was what most people would term a catastrophe. On June 28, 1984, I was diagnosed with cancer. That night the images that rushed through my brain were ones I wanted to erase. My brain kept repeating, 'I've been diagnosed with cancer. I'm going to die.' Disbelief and shock filled me, and I was unable to act, to move...a highly unusual state for me - a woman of action. I was frozen by my fear, trapped by the pictures in my head, and resigned: I was going to die. I collected my thoughts, recapped the memorable snapshots of the past 32 years and started to prepare to die. Death was the only thing I saw. I had one vision - no options - I was stuck. And then it struck me: an overwhelming feeling flooded into my being, and I said, 'Grace, yes, you have cancer, but you don't have to die.' In a flash I realized the real challenge was not dealing with death but creating a life worth living, even if I had Hodgkin's disease. I was still scared - not of dying but of facing the challenge of living.

THUNDERBOLT TRANSFORMATION was born that June night. I wasn't aware of it, of course, but the spark was ignited. The challenge I faced then, and continue to face each day, is not getting stuck. By not letting traditional thinking patterns drive my brain, it allowed me to break out of the mode, see the situation another way. That release unleashed new ideas, energies and strengths. My main business strength stems from what you could call the Thunderbolt motto: Act now! As I said earlier, I've always been a woman of action. I believe in working towards goals, even if I'm not entirely convinced I'm ready to begin. Learning through doing. In my transformation from educator to consultant, I've trusted in my ability to be flexible and to do what needed to be done.

Of course, my other important business strength was knowing when to seek out help through networking, creating emotional and practical supports and contacts in the business world. I've worked most closely with the National Association of Women

Business Owners (NAWBO). My relationship with NAWBO has been mutually beneficial since 1981 when I first did PR for our Pittsburgh chapter. Through NAWBO I learned what I didn't know about myself back in 1981 - that I really wanted to be a business leader. NAWBO opened the door for me with its visionary training of leaders for a world of change. In 1981, I also couldn't articulate what I intuitively knew - that I wanted to develop a supportive business environment. Through the great opportunity of meeting all these outstanding, successful women business owners, I've begun to put my desire into practice; as NAWBO puts it: 'To change the course of management and manage the course of change.' Through NAWBO, I've worked with women business owners coast to coast, developing business leadership and helping members succeed in their own businesses.

It's also through NAWBO that I've learned the advantages of being a woman in business. Although I haven't experienced many of the major disadvantages, one area that's been sensitive for me is my history as a teacher. Because that profession is undervalued and in the 'pink ghetto', I'm touchy about revealing my experience as a special education teacher in business settings.

In the 1990's, women have decided advantages in business because our strength is finally being recognized and valued as an economic force. Women business owners own one-third of all businesses and employ nearly one-half of all employees. And, most importantly to me, women's style of leadership is where all business leadership is headed: creating work environments that maximize everyone's potential.

Since women are coming on strong in business, my advice to new women entrepreneurs is ACT NOW! Set a plan, get going, and take action. Additionally, I advise new business owners to volunteer. It builds good PR, contacts and networks, and establishes your leadership credibility, and gives back some of the advice, support and help every new business owner receives.

The past ten years have been a period of tremendous growth. From conquering cancer to managing cash flow, I've gained a valuable insight about my personal power. GM Consultants continues to stretch me and offers a future promise with just as much excitement.

In 1991 I saw the birth of my new company, The Border Gang, which helps companies move between the United States, Canada, and Mexico by easing financial and operational transitions and inventing market penetration strategies. And in 1993, Duncan (my husband) and I plan to traverse the United States-Canadian border in a single-engine plane and co-author a book about our journey. No matter what my future brings, I just know I'll never get <u>stuck</u> again!

GM CONSULTANTS
530 Hastings St., Pittsburgh, PA 15206
TEL: (412) 661-8325, FAX: (416) 944-0413

40

ZEE CARMAN

NEW DAY ENTERPRISES, INC.

Zee Carman is a special type of woman entrepreneur. She is the Executive Director of New Day Enterprises, a community mental health facility that provides training and employment services for 54 developmentally disabled adults in LaGrande, Oregon. Although she has not risked her own money in a private venture, she conceived the idea and through her tireless effort implemented the plan for Blue Mountain Caskets, a business that has enabled adults with profound physical and mental limitations to reach their highest economic potential. She heard that retarded individuals in California had been building caskets, thought of Oregon's being timber country, and began market research on the idea of forming such a company through New Day Enterprises. In 1990 she applied for and received the only grant given to a non-profit organization from lottery funds in the State of Oregon. Today Blue Mountain Caskets is a fully functional manufacturing company and, due to the vision of one extraordinary woman, adults who formerly played only with toys and color crayons now labor side by side producing a product that gives them pride in themselves and at the same time enhances the local economy.

"There is a silver lining behind every cloud.....

I have always been fascinated with psychology and why people do what they do. I am the Executive Director of a community based mental health agency called New Day Enterprises, Inc. New Day is a non-profit organization that provides residential, training and employment services to 54 mentally handicapped adults in Eastern Oregon. Up until this point, my focus has been on human services and behavioral psychology and then suddenly - I became a business woman! I have worked with developmentally disabled adults for 11 years and it is on their behalf that I became an entrepreneur.

The first position I held with New Day Enterprises was as an on-line staff person working directly with people with disabilities. When the previous Executive Director left and I applied for the job, I had a member of the Board of Directors tell me that I would make a good administrator if only I were a man! This made me more determined than ever to succeed. I have been able to prosper in this job largely because of the people I work with. My staff and the Board of Directors have been supportive and encouraging as well as being willing to allow me to develop new ideas.

Non-profit agencies need to be entrepreneurial and innovative just as much as any business. Most mental health agencies exist to 'do good'. This means that we tend to look at our mission as a moral absolute rather than an economic adventure. When I came to work at this agency, many of our clients had come from living most of their lives in an institution for mentally retarded adults. All of these people have an IQ of 70 or below, are mentally retarded, and many have profound physical limitations as well. They were not involved in real work tasks and would spend their day playing with toys or coloring with crayons. I have had the privilege to work with adults with disabilities and help them help themselves and reach their highest economic potential.

I believe in people. About 40 years ago, parents and family were encouraged to institutionalize their children. Out of sight became out of mind. People with disabilities have become a hidden population. The best way to integrate a hidden population into a community is through the work force. We started small, with one janitorial job and a crew of three disabled adults with a supervisor, and took our folks into the community and into work places. Opportunities were limited and I feel that I have had to help the workers with disabilities prove themselves and their work again and again. Each job opportunity made an impact. I loved seeing what good employment and a paycheck can do.

There is always a point in which personal and professional pieces of our lives merge. Mine resulted in a new business and a brand new career direction. There is a silver lining behind every cloud. It was at my father's funeral in 1988 that the subject of coffins came up. The funeral director was from California and asked me if I knew that retarded adults had built wooden caskets there. It sounded like an interesting idea since wood products are a natural type of production for LaGrande. Northeast Oregon is timber country, and many of the businesses in this area are timber or wood oriented.

I toured an operation that makes caskets, did market research and a feasibility study. In 1990 I applied for a grant to finance the project. I was fortunate to have received one from the Northeast Oregon Economic Development District. They distribute lottery dollars and were looking to finance projects involving secondary wood manufacturing. To date, we are the only non-profit organization in the State of Oregon to receive a grant from lottery funds.

The entire notion of making a traditionally oriented mental health agency into a business is not the norm but made good business sense because of the following reasons:

1. Tax-free status of a non-profit agency is preserved.

2. The business can utilize the agencies' existing Board of Directors and Executive Directors.

3. Space and tools that are not presently utilized.

4. A non-traditional work force of willing, trainable people.

Development of Blue Mountain Caskets has enabled us to provide a quality product at a reasonable price and at the same time create employment for the handicapped. The ripple effect also enhances the economy of our area as we provide more jobs and dollars to the local community.

I was further able to introduce a new concept to the manufacturing process called reverse integration. That is where we hire non-handicapped adults to come in and work side by side with our developmentally disabled workers. Half of the current work force has a physical, mental, emotional or developmental disability. I believe the best way to get anyone to succeed is to focus on their abilities, not their disabilities.

I have a wonderful husband, Tom, and two teenage sons, Jeff and Tony, who are a great behind-the-scenes support system. The best way to be successful in any venture is to fall in love with your job. My husband indulges my love affair with my business. I credit my family for their tolerance when I would discuss at great length the merits of flip-top versus slip-top coffins.

As I was researching the funeral business, I would read the Funeral Director's Handbook and other similar literature before going to bed. It was to try and get a feeling for the business, the language and the point of view of the people who would be customers. I subscribe to magazines like Mortuary Management to keep current with trends and ideas in the industry. I've also been in (yes, in!) the caskets to test for quality control.

I have found that goal setting and having alternative plans for products and marketing strategies have increased my comfort level in beginning a new project. If Plan A doesn't work, I already have Plan B prepared and ready to activate. That way I can adopt, adapt and reject. I plan on using the same plan that was successful for Blue Mountain Caskets to form other revenue producing divisions of our agency.

I wish the best to all women entrepreneurs. My advice is to fall totally, head-over-heels in love with your project. Enjoy whatever point you are at now. Keep a sense of humor, you'll need it! Choose your job, believe in yourself and the time and energy you commit will work miracles. My entrepreneurial efforts have been on behalf of adults with disabilities rather than for a project for a personal business or gain. I would like to see more non-profit agencies move to a business focus. The spirit of women entrepreneurs in all fields has no limits, only possibilities."

Editors' Note: Zee is active in Statewide activities as well as community organizations. She is active in the Chamber of Commerce and the Oregon Rehabilitation Association and is a member of the Rural Access Committee for the Oregon Transportation Plan. She has conducted workshops on various aspects of management issues and human service programs.

NEW DAY ENTERPRISES, INC.
2107 N. Depot Street, La Grande, Oregon 97850
TEL: (503) 963-2348

HELEN SHIH
SHE'S FLOWERS

Helen Shih, the co-founder, CEO and president of She's Flowers, Inc., was born and raised in Taiwan in a middle class family. She received her Bachelor's Degree in Biochemistry in 1975 and then immigrated to the United States. She received her Master's Degree in Biochemistry in 1978 from Occidental College after which she worked as a biochemist and medical technician. In 1979 her brother, Marty Shih, also came to the United States. With $500.00 given to them by their mother, the two rented a closet-sized space and opened a flower stand. Today, She's Flowers, Inc. is a totally computerized full service floral franchise in California. Helen's function is to oversee the financial status of the organization and trouble shoot for the whole operation. In 1989 she also established the Asian Business Connection specializing in servicing the Asian community and networking between Asian business and top fortune companies.

"After several months in the United States and with naive courage, we went into business for ourselves in order to make our entrepreneur dreams come true.....

In 1979 my younger brother, Marty, came to the United States with $500.00 which was given to him by our mother, Mrs. Hsuan-Yann Pei Shih. My mother worked hard all of her life and tried to send all of her four children to the United States to study and to become established and live in this country.

In March of 1979 we found a closet-sized space to rent for $150.00 a month in a downtown office building on Olive Street. The landlord, Mr. Chris Demetriou, wanted a flower stand there. Despite Marty being a Math student and I a biochemist and medical technician, we became instant florists.

We truly believed 'IT DOESN'T MATTER HOW SMALL THE BUSINESS, WE WANT TO START OUR OWN BUSINESS IN THE LAND OF OPPORTUNITY - AMERICA.' We thought that this would allow us to start with the equal opportunity as the native Americans had. A new enterprise could begin despite the cultural background, proficiency in English, and the capital to start a business.

In March 1979, after selling exactly $2.00 worth of flowers on our first day of business, Marty and I stored the remaining flowers in a commercial refrigerator that we had rented. The second day when we arrived at the store, the flowers were all frozen. We were really sad at that time but then Marty and I started to laugh about the lack of knowledge of the flower business. 'TO CONTINUE AN EDUCATION IS ONE OF THE MOST IMPORTANT KEYS TO SUCCESS.'

We have followed our dreams across the Pacific and prospered through determination, hard work and persistence. Marty and I founded She's Flowers in 1979 and throughout our struggles, crushing hard work, and the fun of challenges, we completed the franchise requirements for She's Flowers in 1986. 'WE TRULY BELIEVE WITHIN THIS GREAT AMERICA, IF YOU

WANT TO WORK HARD, EVERYONE WANTS TO HELP.'
We both love this country and the people who share their work
ethics and helping hands with us.

I am the CEO and President of She's Flowers, Inc., which is a
totally computerized full-service floral franchise operation in
California. Currently there are six franchise units in Southern
California. My function at She's is to oversee the financial
status of the organization and be the trouble shooter for the
whole operation.

We discovered that the typical flower shop cannot meet the
tremendous demand for the consumer needs during a holiday
season. We keep learning through our own mistakes and we
created the following unique points which are making us
outstanding in the floral industry:

> The computerized networking system allows us to
> transmit and receive floral orders nationwide and
> worldwide by data processing without relying on
> a human being. It also performs the function of
> daily business accounting that works efficiently.
> This allows us to observe the store performance
> closely in order to keep business alive and stay
> ahead of the competition.

> The systematized and standardized operation
> allows us to simplify the entire floral operation
> system. With a limited number of pre-made
> variety of floral products and customizing floral
> products, this allows us to provide general
> consumers with a wonderful product at a
> reasonable price with the very best in quality and
> service.

> The simplification of operating procedure is the
> key of She's Flowers internal operation. Only a
> simple operation could create a smooth and happy
> environment for people to work there, and with
> continuing education, it could keep us ahead in
> our industry.

We soon transferred the computer network concept to our 777-CLUB, the Asian Business Connection which was established in 1989, with the help and interest of Mr. Chris Demetriou, our former landlord. Mr. Demetriou is the most generous and bright person we have ever met and we frequently consider him as our godfather of our business. 777-CLUB is a telecommunication and telemarketing company specializing in very active networking in Asian business and in the community.

Through our own experiences we understand and realize what types of difficulties the immigrants have either living or doing business in this country. We built up Multilingual Toll-free Telephone Networking Services, 1-800-777-CLUB (2582), to service the Asian communities throughout the United States and to cater to the needs of these immigrants. From this court we start all the functions of Asian business with the top fortune companies.

We position ourselves as a gateway for top fortune companies (MCI, American Express, etc.) to market their services in the growing Asian Market in the United States and Pacific Rims. With the 777-CLUB network, multilingual operators and telemarketers services allow us to successfully reach an ethnic market for these top companies. For example, we are one of the three top sales agencies for MCI in the United States who have successfully developed MCI Asian international and national long distance business. Currently we are finishing the negotiations to be the sales marketing company for American Express. In the meantime, we are working with New York Life and Annuity Co. to build up the financial service needs for Asian communities."

SHE'S FLOWERS INC.
21 S. Venice Blvd., Suite #6, Venice, CA 90291
TEL: (213) 356-7478, FAX: (213) 329-7437

STEPHANIE SLAVIN

AVIATION BUSINESS CONSULTANTS, INC.

Stephanie Slavin is the president of Aviation Business Consultants, Inc., a transportation planning firm specializing in the use of helicopters for transportation and economic growth. The firm consults to develop heliports and helicopter airlines for hospitals, cities, international airports, and office parks worldwide. Stephanie got her private pilot's license at 18. With a college minor in Aviation Technology, she went to work for the FAA advancing from air traffic controller to manager of The Technology Exchange Office. Stephanie fell in love with flying helicopters in 1977, and quickly envisioned their becoming the world's next major transportation system. She has earned phenomenal credibility in the male-dominated aviation world. In 1985 she received a nomination for Presidential appointment to the National Transportation Safety Board; in 1988, she was invited to address two Heli-Network Symposiums in Japan; and in 1989 she presented a paper before the 1989 World Conference on Transportation Research held in Yokohama, Japan. In 1990, Stephanie was invited to testify on the "Civilian Applications of the Tiltrotor" before the House Aviation Subcommittee.

"Listen to your inner voice, choose what you love to do and make that your business.....

Aviation Business Consultants, Inc., evolved somewhat unexpectedly in 1981. However, entrepreneurism had budded several times since adolescence. From age 16-20, I gave piano lessons and produced annual recitals for my students to recognize their musical accomplishments. Next came my lifelong involvement with real estate investment. I bought my first home in college (age 20) because I abhorred paying rent. Having roommates helped pay my mortgage and earn write-offs. I bought a second rental property the next year, and in almost every year thereafter (1970-1980). In college, I sold airplanes, first for a grad student who had a small business, then for my father who opened an aircraft sales business to take advantage of my newly discovered talent/interest in selling. I had grown up flying with my parents, got my private license 3 months after graduating from high school, and earned more ratings while in college. In 1975-78 (while working for the FAA), I also developed and marketed a computerized biorhythm chart. The business had a cable television commercial and ads in major magazines for the 'Biorhythms by Stephanie' chart. In 1983, I financed my Porsche mechanic to move from New Jersey to Florida and, as partners, we opened 'The Black Forest Garage' in Delray Beach, where it is still operating successfully today.

My original plans had been for a career in medicine. At Purdue, I earned a B.S. in Microbiology with a minor in Aviation Technology. Disillusioned by a dramatically unsuccessful laboratory experience which deflated my hypothesis on antibiotics, I opted to take the FAA (Federal Aviation Administration) admission test for air traffic control (ATC). From 1971-1973, I worked in Indianapolis as an air traffic controller. Then I took a job as an analyst writing ATC computer programs at the FAA Technical Center in Atlantic City, N.J. In 1980, I moved to manager of the new Technology Exchange office set up under the Reagan administration. The entire time I worked for the FAA, I would wonder when I was going to work for myself. Finally, in 1981, when I was in the best, most enjoyable position of my career, the federal government austerity program closed my Technology Exchange Office. However, because my job of linking up the FAA's R&D facility with those of industry and government aviation counterparts around the world had been so important, several CEO's in the U.S. aviation industry asked me to continue providing the information. My 8 years of government service had afforded me 'return rights' to a previously held position in air traffic automation, so I accepted that and began 'consulting' to industry while still working for the FAA.

Within three months, I realized (with the help of an astute friend) that I didn't have to continue working for a miserable boss in a tedious job which bored me to tears (ATC automation). So, I quit the FAA, expanded my consulting, and moved from the economically depressed Northeast to business-vibrant Florida to work with a client who wanted to develop a premier fixed-base operation for jets and helicopters at Ft. Lauderdale Executive airport. A few months later, I asked myself 'What would I **really** like to do in aviation with my business?' And, the answer was to be involved with helicopters. Next question was, 'What needs to be done?' Answer: heliports. I joined the Helicopter Association International, went to the FAA's libraries, and talked to helicopter operators. I chose to develop my opportunity into a business to achieve **FREEDOM** (both creative and financial, and to be free of the political inanities of the government's multi-year budgeting process); for **CHOICE**, the ability to do anything I wanted to do and loved, not just what I was told to do; and for **SATISFACTION**, feeling good about being able to immediately solve problems; enjoying working and turning my creativity into benefits for others.

As of 1991, I have been in the aviation consulting business for ten years. My concepts have been developed by constantly asking questions, observing trends, envisioning the future of transportation, then letting that vision guide my business choices. I love to write and speak, and used those abilities to develop credibility and to cost-effectively publicize my unusual business. I have taken advantage of numerous opportunities, but have also offered myself to speak at industry conventions and conferences and write articles for magazines such as the 'China Aviation Journal' etc.

In 1988, I was invited to address two Heli-Network Symposiums in Tokyo and Beppu, Japan, and to present a paper before the 1989 World Conference on Transportation Research held in Yokohama, Japan. As always when speaking, I boldly expressed my consistent theme, that **helicopters would become the world's next major transportation system;** and consequently, depicted our company's product as the 'helicopter transportation system,' rather than as individual heliports, which is what we were actually building (but a single heliport is the foundation of an eventual system). Since the Japanese announced in 1988 their plans to build a nationwide transportation system using helicopters, my peers are acknowledging (some, with surprise/awe) that I have been promoting that concept for years!

The male-dominated aviation world has been an outstanding training ground, teaching focus, self-control, and how to adroitly deal with chauvinism. Being a woman in an unusual profession has rendered me distinctive and memorable, prime for publicity. It has also enabled me to get in to see almost any executive...more than one has told me that he agreed to see me just because he was 'curious' to hear what a woman might have to say. However, being a woman has also had its disadvantages. Men as individuals have been extremely helpful and supportive, but their advice was frequently too narrow in scope for my needs. Men in groups (boards of directors, committees) on the other hand, have been eager to quash the new ideas my company has expounded.

Business and life continue to get better every year. One of the best surprises has been one of the most recent, that of being warmly received by the Japanese. They have made me feel that ideas are more important than gender, while still being most considerate of my gender. In Japan I have been treated as though I head a company of great size and power instead of a 'small business.' In 1985, I was honored by receiving a nomination for Presidential appointment to the **National Transportation Safety Board (NTSB)** from two separate sources. I was invited to testify before the House Aviation Subcommittee in April, 1990, and had my remarks quoted several times by the Congressmen conducting the hearing.

Perhaps the greatest satisfaction comes from observing that the predictions I made when I started the company in 1981...that helicopters would be the next major transportation system; that it would be about 15 years before heliport networks developed in the U.S. (1996); and that the transportation system would probably happen in some other country first...are all coming to pass in the time I had projected. My greatest help has come from within; managing emotions, learning to blend my desire to be warm and giving with the need to be objective. Calling on others for specific help has also been beneficial. A particularly interesting benefit resulted from a friend in the helicopter industry who appointed me to two different industry boards which resulted in increased knowledge and credibility and receiving business from other board members.

Looking to the future, I hope for growth to $50 million by 2000; possibly buying an engineering firm; capital infusion from a foreign company (because companies outside of the U.S. perceive the opportunities for developing helicopter transportation systems better and are more willing to take a $5-$10 million risk with their longer-range vision). We also plan to build a prototype system composed of 5-10 heliports around a city to connect its urban/suburban/exurban areas with helicopters that provide service every 15 minutes via the **Heli-Taxi** and **Heli-Bus** concepts innovated by my company, at a cost comparable to existing auto taxi fares.

My advice to other woman entrepreneurs is to listen to your inner voice, choose what you love to do and make that your business. Write a strategic plan...vision, mission statement, strengths, weakness, opportunities, threats. See obstacles not as brick walls, but as signposts pointing you in another direction. Be flexible...observe what's working, what's not, make subtle (or major) changes until you create the product/service that's right for your societal time--or else be willing to wait for that time! Constantly ask questions of yourself and others; constantly improve the quality of your questions until you're getting the results you want. Observe trends, apply what you have to offer to them. Project the trend that will optimize your business opportunity.

DO ONLY WHAT YOU DO BEST!! Hire other people to do the rest. Hire administrative staff (even if it's just a part-time secretary and/or bookkeeper) immediately, because if you don't have to do what saps your creativity and productivity, you will be able to create several times more business than if you 'saved' that hundred dollars a week. Doing without help is a false economy that undermines many businesses, especially those owned by women. With help, you will also look and feel more professional. Join one or two (but not too many) organizations. Be sure that they are composed of powerful people (those who know who they are and who are constantly growing personally as well as in business). Participate, give of your talents, and you will reap countless rewards. NAWBO (National Association of Women Business Owners) has been the most significant and beneficial organization I have ever joined because it is composed of women who value each other and utilize their contacts and experience to benefit their sisters. Besides making incredible new friends nationwide, I have received national publicity, business referrals, and financial reward. The AVIS television commercial on which I appeared as the owner of my business came because the company contacted NAWBO seeking a woman in Florida with an unusual business. NAWBO'S programs at the national level have also taught me the new paradigm of leadership, expanded my pride in the contributions women have made to the U.S. economy, and have provided a focus which I will use to further change my life as I run for Congress in 1992."

AVIATION BUSINESS CONSULTANTS, INC.
7507 S. Tamiami Trail, Suite 176, Sarasota, Florida 34231
TEL: (813) 921-4941, FAX: (813) 925-4900

PATTY DeDOMINIC
PDQ PERSONNEL SERVICES, INC.

Patty DeDominic is a multifaceted entrepreneur, President of PDQ Personnel Services, Inc., headquartered in Los Angeles, California, which she founded 12 years ago. She also owns T-Square etc..., a one year old business which represents production artists; is a partner in an executive recruiting firm and in an art gallery. Her credits include past presidencies of Women in Management and the National Association of Women Business Owners (Los Angeles). She has served on committees for Small Business and Human Resources for California State Senators and the Assembly, as well as the United States Small Business Administration. Patty is Vice Chair of the Los Angeles Private Industry Council and has served as an advocate for business women and entrepreneurs for the past decade. Patty recently received international honors as Champagne Veuve Clicquot's United States' Business Woman of the Year.

"I believe that business, like life and motherhood, is constant negotiation.....

My business, PDQ Personnel Services, Inc., grew out of my experiences in the work world in the mid-seventies. The doors for women in middle management had been cracked but not yet fully opened. The training I received as a sales manager for a Fortune 500 cosmetics firm, combined with business classes at both USC and UCLA helped me to see that my contributions and accomplishments could be profitable for my own business.

Starting a personnel service was not really what I had originally envisioned for myself. Actually I yearned for a top management spot in a non-traditionally-female company. Interviews with oil companies, printing and advertising firms, even a major distributor usually ended up with me interviewing a lesser experienced man, occasionally receiving job offers below my capacity.

This is when I began meeting with search firms and employment agencies, trying to convince them to place me in some challenging top job. It seemed that most were not qualified to help me and listening to the needs of the applicant was a rare activity.

I had discovered a true need in the market place, employers needing mid-level people and an employment agency that would truly listen and be responsive to applicants' current needs and career aspirations. PDQ Personnel Services was started in 1979 with those idealistic goals. I vowed that no woman would ever be denied an interview for a position she was qualified and prepared for.

Today, PDQ places people in a variety of jobs, both full time and temporary. Our first few years were very difficult. We definitely had to learn many lessons the hard way because I had less than $3,000 in savings to capitalize the company. My experience as a manager in a large company hadn't prepared me for collecting receivables, bank relations and the many other serious responsibilities of business ownership.

58

To round out my education, I took seminars offered by the U.S. Small Business Administration and universities and immediately became involved in professional organizations. These activities exposed me to resources, role models and business contacts. I became President of Women in Management, then the National Association of Women Business Owners, gaining leadership experience and visibility.

PDQ's growth from $136,000 our first year to $15,000,000 twelve years later, with plans to exceed $30,000,000 has been propelled by our commitment to the highest ethics. We know that our ability to evaluate candidates, guide them and give cost effective and prompt service to our client companies is our key to success.

The company has carefully calculated risks and moved forward on innovative ideas for special services. We try to empower each of our employees to make decisions and go out of their way to fully satisfy the customer and solve problems quickly and completely. Being flexible and resilient are essential for business survival and growth in the 90's.

You might wonder how we were able to survive in an already competitive industry. Many of our competitors had been in business for 25 years and there were over 1,000 personnel services in Los Angeles in the '70's. It definitely challenged every ounce of my conviction. I've had to mortgage my house, explain to employees why I would not be able to make payroll and bargain with landlords when rent was due. These business setbacks were painful and embarrassing lessons in the first few years but I vowed to learn from them and become a better planner.

We learned to do annual strategic planning for staff, cash, sales and growth. Today our managers plan on future development of their staff as well as direct the day to day operations. PDQ understands it is important to establish credibility internally and externally. This commitment to professional excellence must go beyond our customer relations and sales efforts. Our reputation as a well run, profitable firm is not only important to our staff but also to our bankers, vendors and the community who refer jobs, candidates, and customers to us.

The recession of 1991 has been another important lesson and validation of business planning. When we lost a $1.5 million contract we had been expecting to win, our plans had to be quickly adjusted and growth strategy switched into the survival mode. But I have found that this multimillion dollar enterprise still requires the basic fundamentals of identifying opportunities, setting and modifying goals and making plans to accomplish those goals. Solving real problems is dependent on identifying the root causes, not just the symptoms, then gathering the people and resources to solve those problems.

I believe that business, like life and motherhood, is constant negotiation; standing firm at times when all odds appear against you yet being willing to make compromises too.

My advice for a new entrepreneur is to persevere. Gather the best advisors, employees and friends to help and guide you in your burning mission. The time for entrepreneurs is truly here with half of all business projected to be owned by women by the year 2000. It won't be easy but the real rewards come to those who keep an open mind to feedback, new opportunities and a far-sighted eye out for obstacles.

Try to keep the other important parts of your life in balance; your family, the community and the spiritual side, not just your business. You'll be a better business and family person for it and when you've achieved stellar financial success, you'll have people you can share it with and the real joys of life."

PDQ PERSONNEL SERVICES, INC.
5900 Wilshire Boulevard, 4th Floor, Los Angeles, CA 90036
TEL: (213)938-3933, FAX: (213)938-2715

VERA MOORE

VERA MOORE COSMETICS

Actress-entrepreneur Vera Moore was born in Corona, Queens, New York. She attended Public School 143, Flushing High School, Hunter College, received a four year scholarship to Sadisburg Academy of Music and studied privately with a professor at Julliard School of Music. She was one of the first black actresses to be contracted on a national television show and portrayed "Linda" on "Another World" soap opera for 12 years. Established in 1979, Vera Moore Cosmetics is now one of the most progressive and prestigious lines for the ethnic market, and offers a comprehensive line of skin care and cosmetic products for the professional and retail market. The company started locally in New York, and their products are currently distributed both domestically and internationally. Today women in every walk of life including models, actresses and entertainers use Vera Moore Cosmetics for its superior quality, make-up lessons and expertise. Vera is a member of NAWBO, One Hundred Black Women, and AWED - American Woman's Economic Development.

61

"I had no idea my acting career would someday lead into creating a cosmetic line for the women of color.....

The need for a quality cosmetic line specifically designed for the ethnic market has long been overdue. Black women were looking for a makeup that was non-greasy, not red and did not rub off on their clothes. I had no idea my acting career would someday lead into creating a cosmetic line for the women of color - Vera Moore Cosmetics.

At the age of six or maybe younger, I was singing in church. I always was vivacious, effervescent and outgoing and had a strong desire to perform and demonstrate the talent that God gave me. I was quite talkative and would always express my opinion. There was no doubt in anyone's mind that the stage was going to be my life. I participated and sang in all the plays in school, at graduation exercises and anything and everything that necessitated being in front of an audience. As the recipient of a four year scholarship out of J.H.S. 127 from Sadisburg Academy of Music in Brooklyn, New York - I was ecstatic.

I was born in Corona (Queens) New York, the youngest of seven children, five brothers and one sister. I knew I had to work extra hard to compete to achieve my goal. My mother was a very strong willed domestic worker. My father was an extremely arduous worker and caring person. The realization of being poor never occurred to me until I was an adult. Only now do I come to understand the incredible sacrifices my parents made for me. I have been extremely blessed and fortunate. I have no sad stories of a broken home, etc. Our parents taught us the true meaning of love, harmony and understanding within the family. I am a product of humble beginnings, however rich in 'love'. 'Put God first and he will direct the path' has certainly been true. All good things will continue to develop by retaining this proverb.

Sadisburg Academy was an exciting experience for me. I studied voice prior to that with our neighborhood voice teachers, Mr. Goffrey and Mrs. Collins. However, Mr. Julia Heinz who taught opera for performers at the Met., etc., also taught 'little me' from Corona, Queens. I knew this scholarship was heaven sent.

Facing reality and setting priorities were components of my life from an early age. Sometimes I truly feel I didn't enjoy life enough, maybe I was too serious (oh well, that's another story). I knew I had to work hard. I needed money even with a scholarship. So during my senior year at high school I took a test for the Federal Government. I did not know they were going to call me two weeks after graduation (no rest for the weary). I graduated in June and started working for United States Customs in July. My plan of action was underway - stay home and save money. I went to acting, singing and drama classes to refine my skills. You must have a plan. It may vary, but at least start out with an idea on paper of what you want to accomplish.

Five years later I left Customs and all those fabulous benefits for a job in the chorus at Guy Lombardo's Jones Beach Theatre. Deep down I guess I was always an entrepreneur at heart - always willing to let go of the trunk of the tree and go out on a limb, from the chorus to small parts, commercials to Broadway, 'Purlie Victorious', 'Treemonisha', etc. As a result of Jackie Mason's 'A Teaspoon Every Four Hours', I got an audition for 'Another World', the soap opera. I auditioned and got it! I was one of the first Blacks to be contracted on national television. A five year contract evolved into a twelve year stay with 'Another World' as Linda Metcalf.

Media unlike stage requires close-ups. Stage as they say is bigger than life, but television comes right into your living room so you want to look absolutely perfect. I didn't. The make-up that was used was heavy, pancake and not appropriate for my skin tone. It was about supply and demand. There were not many Blacks on television, if any, and none in major contract roles. I decided during 'Another World' to come out with a quality line for the women of color.

I needed help. A talented friend, Romania Ford, make-up artist at 'Another World', helped me understand undertones and hues.

The existing Black lines in the department stores weren't doing the job, they were too red and too greasy. The White lines seemed to just add color to their existing line, resulting in wrong consistency for our skin, and everyone looked ashy, gray, or too dark. I hired a chemist and went to work.

Money is always an obstacle especially if you don't have it, so I did it again. I mortgaged my house and got an SBA loan and took two years and developed Vera Moore Cosmetics - The Make-up That Doesn't Rub Off On Your Clothes Or His! The rewards of struggle have been beautiful. Lena Horne, Cosby Show, A Different World, soap operas (of course), movies, etc., are a few that have used Vera Moore Cosmetics. We moved to the Green Acres Shopping Mall in Valley Stream, Long Island in December 1982 and are the first Black tenant in the 40 year history of Green Acres.

None of this would have been possible without my loving husband, Billy, who tolerated my moods (actress-entrepreneur double jeopardy) and was always there when I needed him, and my daughter, Consuella, who understood when I was away from home marketing Vera Moore Cosmetics. My loving family gave me support morally and spiritually in whatever I endeavored.

A very special thanks goes to my sister, Betty, and my aunt, Lois, who are today's Sojourner Truth for me...I Love You!"

VERA MOORE COSMETICS
2034 Green Acres Mall
Sunrise Highway, Valley Stream, N.Y. 11581
TEL: (516) 825-3477

JOANN NOONAN

GOURMET HOUSTON

JoAnn Noonan is the owner and President of Gourmet Houston, in Houston, Texas. Gourmet Houston is a restaurant and corporate catering company, in business now since 1983. JoAnn is a native Californian who turned a lifelong love of food, cooking and travel into her livelihood. She has a degree in English literature and a graduate degree in Education. JoAnn's first venture was a dinner party service for friends that combined her cooking skills with flexible hours. She cooked at home in her kitchen, lugged the food to the party, served and cleaned up. Years later, she decided to market her skills in a more commercial arena that would allow her financial independence. JoAnn bought Gourmet Houston and has transformed it from "utter chaos" to a smoothly run operation. Today, she takes pride in her team of professionals and an extensive clientele list. Best of all, she makes money doing her own thing in the field she loves.

65

"I've cooked since I could walk so I decided to try my hand at cooking for others.....

I've always wanted to own my own business. Maybe it was something I was born with, an offbeat gene, I don't know. I do know now that entrepreneurial characteristics tend to run in families, like blue eyes and left-handedness, and my family certainly follows the profile. My father left corporate America at age 55 to become a commercial realtor and opened his own firm. My paternal grandmother had a beauty salon in Hollywood, California, while I was growing up, and my maternal great grandmother came from Minnesota to Long Beach, California, in the early days of this century. As a widow with children to raise, she opened a boarding house and ended up owning it and several other nearby pieces of real estate. My brother is a dentist in his own practice in Washington State. We joke that we're in business for ourselves because no one else would have us! Some truth to that, and therein lies both the strength and weakness of our entrepreneurial maverick minds.

So why did I actually go into my own business and how did I start? It wasn't because of my education. I have a degree in English literature and a graduate degree in Education. I taught school long enough to know I loved the people contact but not the job of teaching. I wanted to return to work after my children were born and I had an overwhelming desire to make money doing my own thing in a field I loved. And one of my life's passions is food. I've traveled a lot and I love foreign as well as American cuisine. I've cooked since I could walk, and so I decided to try my hand at cooking for others. I called my friends who entertained and told them that if they wanted to really enjoy their next dinner party to let me do all the work. I named my new enterprise 'The Joy of Not Cooking'. I cooked at home, lugged all the fixings to the party site, served and cleaned up.

The business was on a roll when I suddenly had to put it on hold. My husband was offered a transfer to Rio de Janeiro. I didn't mind the travel, but it was hard to leave my growing business behind. While we were there, I tried to make the best of my new world. I studied Portuguese and became fluent. Three years later, my family and I ended up in Houston. I realized that the days of endless summers were over and decided to begin catering again. After my marriage ended, I was ready to move into commercial catering so I could become independent.

I went to work for a local caterer for $5.00 an hour and, after two months she offered to sell me the business. I made her an offer, which she refused, so I quit and spent six months researching business opportunities. I looked at start-ups, franchises, partnerships and ended up with a lot more education, back where I started, and after two more offers, bought Gourmet Houston in August of 1985, six years ago.

I knew nothing about running a business, but I had organizational skills, I love people, and as a woman I had a skill many men are socialized out of - I wasn't afraid to ask for help. One of the reasons I bought Gourmet Houston was because it had good accounting records. Most small businesses don't. I had information about the company's finances, even though at the beginning I couldn't read a balance sheet or a P & L. So I worked with my accountant and with my father on the financial side of the business. I worked with Don, my life partner, learning managerial skills, how to hire and fire, delegate, hold meetings, motivate, in short, how to build a team. I built a support network that included vendors who would give good service to a small account, a repairman I could afford who could come at a moment's notice to repair the ancient walk-in cooler before all the food spoiled, a plumber, an attorney, etc.

I found out over time what I was good at. I built a team of people with specific interconnecting jobs instead of the mass confusion I inherited. I cut costs till it hurt and settled interpersonal disputes with frequent staff meetings where everyone could air gripes and test solutions. I'm not good at marketing. I've periodically struggled with it, taken courses, gritted my teeth while I cold-called catering prospects. So wisely, I think, I have just hired my first professional PR person, another important support link at this time in our history.

In 1986 and 1987, shortly after I bought Gourmet Houston, Texans started feeling the economic slide that was in motion for several years. People stopped spending money on social events. At about the same time, I was becoming a little burned out on having to spend every weekend on the job, so I decided to look at the slump in a positive way. I figured there were two directions I could go. One, to compete harder for the scarce social events or two, concentrate on corporate catering. I chose the latter and it's worked out great. We're not as diversified now as other catering companies but we're centered, and I have the opportunity to spend more time on the weekends travelling and relaxing.

On occasion we've run into a few problems as does any restaurant. One horrifying moment was when the chef accidentally put green peppercorns, instead of capers, into a batch of caponata. It was right before a party, so we got out the plastic gloves and picked every single peppercorn out of the mixture.

My worst memory, though, was five years ago when Gourmet Houston was still handling social catering. My staff and I were at a private home for a Christmas party when the chef realized during the entree service that he had forgotten the dessert at the restaurant. I rushed back, speeding about 80 on the Southwest Freeway, when suddenly I was pulled over, not by one, but two Houston police officers. I begged them to follow me to the restaurant and write the ticket on the way, but they wouldn't go for it. I had to wait for the ticket but I still somehow managed to get the dessert to the party on time. Incidents like that should give you a clue as to why I stopped doing social catering.

At this point in time I've gained enough confidence in myself and my staff to begin to grow larger as well as better. With some expert marketing and publicity assistance I plan to work toward doubling my company's sales in the next three or four years, and move our rather humble facility to newer, more upscale surroundings. Would I do it again? You bet. I've become financially independent. I've developed my company's reputation for quality and honesty. I can make things happen.

I can solve problems and handle crises in a positive way. I would advise any woman considering starting a business to do it! You never know what you're capable of until you try. Keep in mind a few things as you go. First of all, develop a business and financial plan. Ninety percent of new businesses fail; the major reasons are undercapitalization and lack of management skills. Get expert help in the areas you are weak in, and expect to pay for it. Learn how to deal with your employees so a team spirit is developed and everyone feels his contribution is vital to the company's success. And I hope that you discover, as I did, that the person 'nobody else would have' has made that uniqueness into a grand and profitable asset!"

GOURMET HOUSTON
809 Studemont, Houston, TX 77007
TEL: (713) 862-8678, FAX: (713) 862-8691

CAROLINE NAKKEN & SANDRA COTTEN
SPI - SUNSHINE PROMOTIONS, INC.

Caroline Nakken, President and Sandra Cotten, Vice President are sisters-in-law. Their company, Sunshine Promotions, Inc. is a Southern California in-store direct marketing agency specializing in product promotions. SPI was founded in Phoenix, Arizona in 1976 as Sunshine Company and incorporated in 1981 as Sunshine Promotions, Inc. What started out as a one-man show in a room at home has grown to be a multi-million dollar corporation. Caroline's background included waitress, gas attendant, flight attendant, ski lift operator, safety equipment sales person, convention hostess and two years of college. At 22 years of age she landed in Phoenix where she started Sunshine Company. Sandra's background in business started at the age of 21 as an administrative aide at USC where she was directly responsible for food, housing budget, and payroll personnel. She continued to manage everything from travel agencies to flower shops for other people until 1978 when she joined forces with Caroline, who is her sister-in-law, to create what is now Sunshine Promotions, Inc. The dream for both was to have the opportunity to create and to have the freedom to direct their own destiny. Caroline, with a creative side and an abundance of energy, and Sandra, having the business logic and background, were a perfect balance.

"After all, she can only be getting five calls a week.....

SPI specializes in promotions in retail stores. The majority of our promotions include in-store samples and coupons. Demonstrators set up tables next to the product they are promoting and either prepare samples and/or pass out coupons. Reports are submitted to the office indicating price, product sold, number of consumers and general customer comments. These reports are summarized and submitted to the client. National brands, as well as local and regional products, use SPI locally and Mass Connections nationally to reach their consumers.

The corporate office houses twenty full-time employees who in turn contract to forty-five areas and six thousand independent contractors.

The primary focus of our business is to introduce, educate and excite consumers about the products we represent. Unlike other forms of advertising, in-store promotions generate immediate sales results.

Enough of the statistics. Let's get on to the real story of this partnership. Let's go back to when I (Sandy to my friends) got introduced to this gorgeous, sexy hunk of a man by my next door neighbor who just happened to be his sister. Of course, when he finally introduced me to the rest of the family, they were all just as beautiful. Especially one particular sister called Caroline. She was one of your 'typical beautiful blond types'. You know, the ones that have three dinner dates on the same night and pull it off. Or the type that guys make appointments with to bring by their Christmas presents.

Two children and five years later for me and who knows how many adventures for Caroline, I heard about the business Caroline was struggling with in Phoenix. She decided to bring it to Southern California and really give it a good chance in a bigger market.

It wasn't until after she had been out here awhile
became involved. Okay, 'I'll put a phone in my spare b
for the business'. Now how much trouble can that be.
after all, she can only be getting five calls a week.
You can't imagine how many times client's were told that those
noisy kids in the background were really the copy machine that
had just jammed.

I remember the first Las Vegas convention. Caroline and I both
left town thinking what can go wrong. We've only got five
people on jobs this weekend and we're really not too far away.
Wrong again. How about three out of the five not showing up.
Decision: guess we both won't go out of town again at the same
time.

In order to have capital to grow, it was decided after three
years to incorporate. How do you do this when you're as small
as we were? It's called 'friends and family', those with the
talents to guide you and those that have the money to make it
happen. There were easily a dozen or more friends and family
that helped us with badly needed loans and extra hands.
However, there were a few special ones that stood out. One
was Marty Gooen, United Business Investors, who was well
versed in the buying and selling of businesses. A good friend,
intrigued with our unique operation, he guided us, counselled
and assisted us in our incorporation. Candice Lincoln who had
worked for Caroline in Phoenix, and wanted to become a
partner, bought into thirty percent of the business which
offered us the opportunity for growth, (an office, equipment,
personnel and sales material). She sold out early due to
personal financial problems to Caroline's Dad. Mom and Dad
Gwynn (my parents) have always been there to lend money,
time or support whenever needed. And last, but two of the
most important, have been Mom and Dad Cotten who helped
with loans and who allowed Caroline to live with them because
there were no paychecks in the early years. His help in
constructing demo tables, convention props and building out one
of our office facilities saved us many dollars and hours.
Unfortunately, due to special reasons, three of these people are
no longer involved in our lives but they will always be an
intricate part of our history. One of our greatest

accomplishments is the fact that the company has repaid all of the personal loans made from friends and family, and with interest as high as 24%.

So now we're incorporated. In the process we rented a small office (of course only one of us could fit in it so I still worked at home), and in the course of it we acquired an attorney. We're in the big leagues now. Good ole John What's his name. We paid him off in liquor that we were purchasing at our demos. We thought it would help sales and make us look better and we needed Christmas gifts for the clients anyway. The last we heard, John was serving drinks to the tourists in the Caribbean.

On to bigger and better things. Our first real shot at a big name; one so big we won't mention it here. Here we are now doing at least 100 promotions a weekend and we get a chance to get on the map. First tryout goes without a flaw. They love us. Second tryout - whoops. But how were we to know that the guy was a pervert. He's done many promotions for us before and not once has anyone complained about him kneeling on the toilet in the women's restroom and looking underneath at the woman in the stall next to him. Well it was fun while we had the account. Guess we'll just have to try for another.

Through the years there have been many stories and situations that have kept this business interesting and challenging. How about the time the demonstrator showed up at the store, ordered pizza and had it delivered to the store. He then sat down on a lounge chair with his family and ate in front of the customers. Needless to say the store manager threw him out. Then he had the nerve to get so mad when we wouldn't pay him for the job that he drove to the office and threatened bodily harm. Guess we can write that payment off to health insurance.

Each year for us has been one of new adventures, new problems and new solutions. It's an ever changing industry we're involved in but really no different than any other. We've continually grown larger and strived to become involved in our industry and help it grow. We created the NADC (National

Association of Demonstration Companies) now over 100 strong. Caroline has served on the board for the Long Beach Sales Club, the Southern California Grocers Advisory Board, NADC and as a Hilite of the Illuminators and is current Executive Vice President of Mass Connections, a national marketing company. I am currently serving as Vice President of the CDA (California Demonstration Association), Illuminators Committee Chairman, working on legislation in Sacramento to help this industry and am President of Mass Connections. We are now getting ready to make our fourth move to larger office facilities.

None of this could have been achieved without the partnership relationship maintaining its strength and energies, or without the support and strength of the many who have helped us over the years. Our special thanks go to our husbands and children who have put up with the late hours, no dinners, no clean clothes or the just plain missing mom because she's working or out of town. Without their support and understanding, SPI would not exist.

We cannot emphasize enough that if you will stay self motivated, persistent and promise not to stop short of your dream through the concessions, sacrifices, long hours and rejections of being in business for yourself, the joy, rewards, self esteem and satisfaction you will achieve are equal to no greater feeling than the birth of a child.

First a state - then a nation. Hey Caroline - do you even know how to speak French? Oh well, here we go again!

SPI - SUNSHINE PROMOTIONS, INC.
720 N. Valley St., Suite M, Anaheim, CA 92801
TEL: (714) 535-8910, FAX: (714) 535-8979

MARTY MASCHINO

ATTIC BABIES

Marty Maschino, founder and president of Attic Babies, a large doll manufacturing company in Drumright, Oklahoma, is the epitomy of the American woman's dream of turning a hobby into a business. Marty began by making dolls which she sold at craft shows. Her business has grown under her loving care into a 15,000 square foot operation that produces approximately 9,000 dolls per week. Marty designs each doll and has been rewarded for her efforts with many honors and with the loyalty of her employees. In 1990 she was named as Oklahoma's Small Business Person of the Year. She was also invited to the White House to present Mrs. Bush with a special edition 'Attic Baby' which she designed as a characterization of the first lady. Marty is the mother of five children, a strong community leader, and (according to her co-workers) a unique lady who exhibits extraordinary creativity, a wonderful sense of humor, and a genuine love for people.

"I am one of those very fortunate people who has been able to have love and laughter as a way of life in both my home and my work......

I am the president and founder of **Attic Babies**, a manufacturing company that started in my home. We now employ 115 workers and manufacture 9,000 dolls per week. The hand-crafted dolls are made of muslin and wear antique clothing characterizing their humorous names. They range in size from 4-inch tall 'little bitty babies' to a life-size 5 foot 8 inch display doll. Each doll is just a little bit different because the faces are hand-crafted. I look for ways to make life funny; that's what keeps the dolls going - the comedy in life.

I was born in Oklahoma City and studied commercial art at Central State University. After my school years, I held positions such as interior designer, artist for a department store chain, and also free-lanced as a commercial artist. During the next few years, our family moved frequently to small towns in Kansas and Oklahoma. Arts and crafts were a natural extension of my education. I made various craft items, including some dolls. The dolls sold immediately and it soon became apparent that they had a ready market.

In 1986, I started my first home-based business. I was making about five-hundred dolls per month and selling them at art & craft shows. This was the beginning of a much larger market.

In July 1987, the first sixteen 'Attic Babies' were sent to the Dallas Wholesale Gift Market for their first national exposure. Thousands of orders rolled in from that summer's gift markets. I hired ten women 'homeworkers' to help me with the increased work of cutting, sewing, stuffing, and dressing of Attic Babies. I finished them and shipped them to the customers.

By October, fifteen additional women were hired and I was designing new dolls as fast as possible for the next gift markets. We moved into our first building, a storefront in Cushing, Oklahoma. It was used partly for storage.

In November of 1987, Attic Babies moved into a 3,500 square foot facility and took our homeworkers with us. For the first time, our workers had designated jobs and responsibilities. We grew and prospered with 1988 sales increasing eight times those of 1987. In March of 1988, we incorporated and moved again, this time into a 9,000 square foot building. Then, in August of 1989, we moved into our new factory in Drumright, Oklahoma, a 15,000 square foot building with a separate office building to accommodate over 100 employees. 'Attic Babies' were now available in all 50 states and internationally. This last move to our current facility was complete with fanfare and keys to the city. Many dignitaries including the Governor and First Lady attended our celebration.

In 1990, I was chosen as Oklahoma's Small Business Person of the Year. Earlier in that same year, I was invited to Washington D.C. where Mrs. Bush was presented with a special edition Attic Baby which I designed as a characterization of the First Lady. She was crafted and detailed with tender loving care, reflecting massive research on the first lady's--and President Bush's--preference for clothing and accessories. Every person in the factory got to put a stitch or two on the doll. A contest was held among the employees and the winning name, 'Grammy Bar', was given to the doll. She now lives in the White House. In September, 1990, I was commissioned by McCalls Pattern Company to design four doll patterns for their pattern books. Four new patterns will be out soon for the fall of 1991.

As a little girl, I had dreams of owning an old-fashioned candy store. That dream was fulfilled with the opening of Fatty Matty's Gourmet Goodies Store, specializing in gift items and old-fashioned candy. Naturally, the main gift attraction is a complete line of Attic Babies. In addition to Attic Babies I have a multitude of other interests and commitments. First on that list would be my five children; Andrew, Christopher, Jennifer, Timothy and Samuel. I serve on several committees and boards and am very active in many civic organizations. I strongly believe in community involvement. Throughout the office and at home, I try to bring a sense of humor that keeps Attic Babies fresh and revived. I design them all--and I retire them when they have lived their lives. I love every one of these Attic Babies. Their personalities resemble little impish kids, all like extensions of my own children. They have a mischievous quality about them. I even named some of the dolls for myself. 'Fertile Myrtle' is me because I have my five children. I laugh at myself and get joy from bringing my creations to life. I have the best of both worlds, a home life and a business that are full of joy and laughter and loving people."

ATTIC BABIES
P. O. Box 912, Drumright, Oklahoma 74030
TEL: (918) 352-4414, FAX: (918) 352-4767

JOYCE McLAUGHLIN
INTERSTATE TELE-MARKETING, INC.

Joyce McLaughlin, owner of Interstate Tele-Marketing, operates an 800 center in Omaha, Nebraska. Joyce married at 17 and had three sons by the time she was 22. In 1971, with no formal education, she went to work for Ambassador Leather Goods as a customer service representative. After six years she was promoted to Manager of Arizona National Marketing Direct Response Center in Omaha, Nebraska and told to "start an 800 center". Her response was, "What's an 800 number?" The center was successful, but subsequently sold and Joyce resigned. A friend encouraged her to start her own company with his money and her know how. Joyce is a woman of goals, all of which she has met. She is currently serving on the National Executive Board of National Association of Women Business Owners as Vice President of Finance. Joyce says, "Superwoman is dead!" Considering her accomplishments, we're not so sure of that.

"I truly believe everyone, man or woman, has the same opportunities. How, where and what we do with them is up to each of us.....

My career really began in 1971. I married in 1960, at age 17, started a family right away and by 1965 had three sons. In 1961 my husband and I moved from New York to Southern California and while having babies, took college prep courses at the local junior college.

After ten years of marriage, my husband and I divorced (only to remarry in 1984 which is another whole story) and moved myself and my sons to Arizona. In September of 1971 I went to work for Ambassador Leather Goods, a mail order company. I started in customer service, was promoted first to the finance department, then to supervisor of Inspection and Quality Control, then to assistant manager in charge of several departments.

In 1977, Ambassador promoted me to Manager of Arizona National Marketing Direct Response Center in Omaha, Nebraska. Ambassador flew me to Omaha, took me to a building they had rented, introduced me to a supervisor, and said, 'Start this 800 center'. I replied 'What's an 800 number?'. That's how much I knew about the industry. Unfortunately, I was not alone, nobody at Ambassador knew anything about running an 800 center and my boss was 1500 miles away. I was really thrown to the wolves.

Luckily, Northwestern Bell representative, Teresa Laughlin, was assigned to my account. She had a little more knowledge than I did but what was most important was that she had access to answers we needed. She took me by the hand and led me, step by step, through the telemarketing mine field. Basically, we learned together. We saw each other daily and because of her ability to obtain answers and my ability to learn, we worked wonderfully together.

Within six short months I became a five star general. Inbound telemarketing is an exciting, ever-changing industry. I found working with statistics, costs (by day), and various other detailed areas challenging. I felt I found my calling.

In 1979 Ambassador decided to sell the center. They asked me to remain as manager but due to a clash in management styles with the new owner, I resigned after two months.

After a short stint trying to help an already-too-far-gone 800 service, I pursued other interviews that took me out of Nebraska. Having uprooted my sons in 1977, I was very concerned about another location change. My sons at that time were 12, 14 and 16, and I felt these were vulnerable years for them, especially being a single parent. After holding a family discussion, we decided to stay in Omaha.

A friend, Lowell Gratopp, who was also my insurance agent, knew of my problem finding a good paying job in Omaha and suggested I start my own 800 business. I knew it would take an investment of $200,000 to $250,000 to start an 800 company and, of course, I did not have the money. Being a novice and not knowing about bank loans, business plans, or the services available from SBA, I only knew how to look for a job.

Again my friend mentioned that I should start my own business. My reaction was, 'Do you have $250,000 you want to invest?' He responded, 'I might!!!' The long and short of it was we took a chance, became 50-50 partners - his money, my brains - and opened Interstate Tele-Marketing in 1980.

In the 800 business, it is very difficult to plan at best beyond two years, and with a new company you plan one year at a time. Our first year we lost $60,000, exactly as I projected. Our second year we showed a small profit and our third year a little larger profit. At that point I knew I would succeed.

I then set my professional and personal goals. Goal setting I learned early in my career at Ambassador. We were constantly establishing goals for production and goal setting became second nature. Of course, women with families set goals all the time but we call them schedules and plans.

My goals were: by 1985 I would buy controlling interest in ITM; my partner would be paid back, with interest, all the money he invested; I would be in the salary range of $50,000 and I would expand ITM into the fulfillment business. I reached all of the goals targeted for 1985 in 1985.

In December of 1986 I suffered a personal set-back in the form of a heart attack. I'm very happy to say I survived. However, I took four months off to recover. This happened to be at the busiest time of the year - the first quarter of the year. Fortunately, my staff came through. I learned I have caring, dedicated, loyal and dynamic people working for me. Not only did ITM survive, 1987 was our highest profit year.

When I started ITM, six people worked 24 hours a day, seven days a week. I was one of those six. For the first 6-8 months I worked in the trenches with my staff. This gave me a chance to get to know them personally, and they in turn learned that I knew what I was doing.

I think my strengths lie in motivating others, having an eye for detail, being a good delegator, understanding the needs of others and working well with them. My general accounting knowledge is good. Although nobody likes to think they have weaknesses, we all do. I sometimes expect people to do things my way, I have a tendency to rush people, I expect perfection, and I assume people know what I know. I am working on improving these areas.

My philosophy was to pay my people well, sometimes more than myself, and to give them responsibility. Those that cared about getting the job done properly are those who moved up. One of the things I'm looking into now is ESOP (Employment Stock Ownership Program). There are a lot of good people who work for me and I feel they should have a vested interest in the company.

When we started ITM, we specifically chose to market ourselves to the small and medium size accounts. There are plenty of 'big guys', centers that can handle 300,000-400,000 calls a day. Our peak is 15,000 calls a day. Because we identified this niche in the market, our competition is minimal. Also, we have a good relationship with the large telemarketing companies. We send clients too big for us to handle to the big guys and they send us the ones that are too small for them.

Because we handle smaller accounts, we are big on customer service. We really try to take care of our clients and the consumer. If we find that a client isn't taking care of its consumers, we're not afraid to cancel an account. Why should we spend our time taking customers' orders just so someone else could ignore them?

In all of my working years, I have had two true mentors. The first, Harry Schneider, I met when I started working at Ambassador. He was Vice President of Operations; he pushed me to the max, challenging me up one side and down the other. He taught me how to delegate, by giving me tasks he knew I could not do alone; he challenged my intelligence by assigning me jobs I had only a vague knowledge of; he gave me the authority to make management decisions and taught me how to handle and accept those decisions, even if they were sometimes wrong; and he challenged my ability by piling more departments on me until I yelled 'uncle'.

Harry believed in me. He didn't see my limits, only my potential and promise. What Harry taught me is evident in everything that ITM does and is. Even when he had his own company, he continued challenging me to expand my horizons up until the time he passed away.

As a typical New Yorker (if you know what I mean), and having come from a male dominated industry with a male mentor, I was not quite the 'lady'. Carol Corey, who is my mentor and friend, helped me smooth out some of my rough edges. She taught me to listen (not always to speak), to have patience, to look toward and think of tomorrow, and to appreciate who I am. She also helped me to try to rid myself of my New York 'slang'.

ADVISE - Many of us are in, or starting a business for different reasons; we inherit them, we need a hobby (something to do to fill our time), we feel we can make a difference in a particular industry, we see a need for our specialty, we need the additional income, we want to make the decisions, we want to be the BOSS, etc. Whatever the reason:

* **Have a plan, do your homework, investigate your competition**
* **Have different financial options**
* **Set time frames and goals**
* **Control expenses**
* **Hire the right people/person - you can't do it alone (part-time help)**
* **A CPA, attorney and banker are a must**
* **Seek out mentors/advisors who have been there**
* **Don't expect great things immediately - BE REALISTIC.**

I truly believe everyone, man or woman, has the same opportunities. How, where, and what we do with them is up to each of us. I know that women business owners face problems. But, do we require special treatment? No! We are not treated the same as men, but do we want to be? No!

We are the force of the future! **Our** success is greater than men! **We** are employing 60% of the workforce! **We** are contributing **billions** to our city, state and national economy. We are not just women business owners...*WE ARE BUSINESS OWNERS WHO ARE WOMEN!!! SUPERWOMAN IS DEAD, BE YOU!!!*"

INTERSTATE TELE-MARKETING, INC.
230 S. 108th Avenue, Suite 2, Omaha, NE 68154
TEL: (402) 333-1900

RUTH CHALOUX BORNAND
BORNAND MUSIC BOX COMPANY

Ruth Chaloux Bornand is 90 years young and still very much the proprietor of Bornand Music Box Company in Pelham, New York. She was born October 13, 1901, in New York City, and moved to Pelham in 1903. On October 12, 1929, Ruth married Adrian V. Bornand, the son of Joseph and Milca Bornand. Adrian graduated from the University of Neuchatelle in Switzerland, returned to Pelham and learned the music box trade from his father who was one of a family of Swiss music box manufacturers. The Bornands restored music boxes for the next several years. Then in 1946 Ruth's spirit of entrepreneurship surfaced. The long hidden thought of putting music box music on phonograph records became a reality. By herself she took a music box to New York City, had it recorded onto an acetate disc, found a pressing plant in Pelham and an artist to do an album cover. For the first time, people who did not have music boxes could enjoy the lovely music and recall memories of an era that was past. Adrian died in 1949 and Ruth continued to carry on the family heritage and still collects, buys, sells and repairs these machines and records their sounds on records and tapes. As a matter of fact, if you were to call Pelham, New York today, you would hear, "Hello, Bornand Music Box Company" spoken by a very lovely lady of 90 who is warm, intelligent and young at heart.

I have many many times been asked, 'How did you get into this Music Box Business?' My husband Adrian, under the strict tutelage of his father, Joseph Bornand, a Swiss trained music box restorer, soon became an expert in this field. His reputation had spread and he soon had many music box repairs. However, this all happened during World War II, when he was manufacturing parts for the Navy, so the repairs had to wait.

Then, back in 1946, when hearing the music box music over the air (at the request of radio station WFAS) and all the response it brought forth, a long hidden thought of mine took shape. I would put the music on phonograph records so many people could know and understand these lovely melodies. I knew nothing about producing records, but for a start, took some of our boxes to the G. Shirmer recording studio in New York City. Well, it was a tremendous experience. In those days, the music was put on an acetate blank - any noise meant that the disc was spoiled and we had to start all over. It was a long trying session, but I did have three good masters.

Fortunately, there was a small pressing plant right here in Pelham. Next, I had to find an album manufacturer and supply the art work. I was again fortunate in locating a firm where they were very helpful, and my 'OLD MUSIC BOX MELODIES' came to life.

Their success was truly amazing - I carried my very amateurish (black and white) album, called 'The Original Music Box Medley of Christmas Songs', to New York City and met with interest from the most prestigious music shops and music department of the large department stores. By the end of the day, I had orders from Wanamaker's, Bloomingdales, Magnovax and Doubleday. One 5th Avenue department store had an outdoor speaker and played the record there. It was amazing to see the number of people who stopped, listened, then went into the store to inquire 'What is that lovely music'? I returned to

Pelham with orders for over 225 albums. Everywhere I played a record, the response was the same, 'Such beautiful music! What is it'?

To go on and on telling of my wonderful responses and experiences would take many pages, so sufficient to say, the first album was reviewed by many of the then prominent music publications and newspaper reviews. I wrote up a circular describing the Music Box music on records.

I began receiving orders from Philadelphia, Washington, St. Louis, Chicago and Neiman-Marcus in Dallas, Texas, who sent a moving truck to Pelham to borrow a supply of music boxes, which were displayed in their store and played over the air. It was very exciting of course, and most gratifying that now the public could hear the wonderful works of the long gone Swiss musicians and craftsmen.

In the meantime, my father-in-law, Joseph Bornand became ill and suddenly passed away. We missed him a great deal, but Adrian was then expert enough to carry on with the repairs, and I went ahead with my recordings.

Again, tragedy struck and Adrian became seriously ill and passed away in 1949. This of course created a vast difference in our lives. Of course I could not carry on the machine shop work. It meant disposing of our building and finding a new home for the girls and myself. This I was able to do by another stroke of good luck. A ten room house with a connecting office was offered to me. It seemed ideal and I immediately purchased it. When my daughters saw the office, one of them said, 'Now mother you can keep all your music boxes in the office rooms and we can use our living room like real people'.

My recordings kept me very busy, until one day I had a visit from Mr. Emile Favre - a descendant of the famous Emile Favre who invented the 'comb', still used in all music boxes. It was just another stroke of good luck, I will call it, that was following the record success. I was then able to continue the repair work with the help of Mr. Favre, and two or three of the good friends Adrian had helped in the music box business. It was amazing to me then, and even now, how the publishing of the music box records changed my whole life.

Just before his death, Adrian and I, with Lloyd Kelley, a music box repairer, decided we would like to form a music box group of friends and customers. The aims and purpose of this group were to acquaint the public with music boxes, their history and care. We founded what was then called the Musical Box Hobbyists, with 22 couples, in late 1949 and it has grown internationally. We have formed 10 chapters throughout America with a membership of approximately 2800.

Also, I will state here that in the early 1900's, the introduction of Mr. Edison's phonograph, called the 'talking voice' really cut down on the sale of music boxes in this country. The golden age of music boxes in America had begun around 1875 and now the industry was dead. Everyone wanted to hear the 'talking voice'.

But the phonograph was the means of bringing my music back to the public on standard 10" records. I went along with the trend of the recordings from there to the 45 RPM records, to the 12" LP records and finally to the cassette tapes of all five albums. I was even approached by Columbia Records and they did my 45 RPM pressing. However, they seemed to be lost in the shuffle at Columbia, so I continued to handle them direct myself along with the others. In this way we accumulated a large list of Music Box enthusiasts of both repairs, buyers and record collectors. Our card files now total over 40,000 names.

I am very grateful for all the success I have had throughout these years, and am still enjoying my music boxes and recordings. My efforts have brought forth a large number of friends and interesting people. I often say my start was partially because I happened to be in the right place at the right time."

EDITOR'S NOTE: According to Mrs. Bornand, the earliest music boxes were made in Switzerland in the late 1700's and early 1800's, and were small, intricate pieces. As time went on, the mechanism became ever more complicated and elaborate, until by 1880 or so, wealthy Americans were buying large furniture-sized music boxes. Mrs. Bornand's music boxes numbering in the hundreds range from small conventional Swiss boxes to table models with interchangeable cylinders and a Regina 69 inch high automatic changer disc box. Her most complex music box was made in Germany in the early to mid-1800's. It plays three discs simultaneously, with a different part of the music on each disc making it sound so rich and melodic that it begins to sound like a full orchestra. She was so impressed with that box, called the Symphonion, which is not for sale, that she recorded 24 of its songs for a record album and now has it on tape.

As another note of interest, I (Linda Pinson) was a clock repairer and music box dealer by trade from 1979 until 1987 when our publishing business required me to give it up. I dealt with Mrs. Bornand during those years when she restored antique music boxes for our shop and our customers. We have also sold her wonderful tapes and records for many years. She is a most unique lady and I feel honored that she took the time to contribute her profile to our book.

BORNAND MUSIC BOX COMPANY
139-4th Ave., Pelham, N.Y. 10803
TEL: (914) 738-1506

O. MONA TOLIN

TOLIN BUSINESS APPRAISERS

As a Certified Business Consultant and a Certified Business Appraiser, O. Mona Tolin buys and sells businesses. Starting with a beauty supply store she owned at age 18, Mona had three businesses before she realized it was buying and selling she loved the most. As owner of Tolin Business Appraisals in Tustin, California, Mona specializes in service businesses, preschools, senior care facilities, and small manufacturing and distribution concerns. She has survived the death of a grown child and the loss of a business to arson; however, she still believes in a positive attitude and hard work. Mona is President-Elect of Orange County NAWBO and the founding member of two organizations, the Business Brokers Association of Southern California, and the Business Opportunity Council of California. She is also an exemplary American patriot. Mona's profile would not have been complete without her story of the adoption of 11 young men and one girl who fought in Saudi Arabia during Operation Desert Storm.

"There are no problems in life, only challenges to be surmounted.....

I have had four businesses in my lifetime, all different, starting with a beauty supply store I opened in Los Angeles at age 18. Many surprises and experiences, some painful and even tragic, have happened along the way. However, I learned early a positive attitude can make life joyous and rewarding. It was my grandmother who said: 'There are no problems in life, only challenges to be surmounted. Mona, always make your own decisions.' This advice stuck with me and helped me to be a survivor and to continue to seek out new opportunities and experiences.

I operated my beauty supply store until I was 28 when I packed up my supplies and household and followed my new husband to Malaysia. I went into the jungle kampongs and, through an interpreter, taught classes to the Chinese, Malaysians, and Indians. We spent four years in Malaysia and when we came back I needed to earn money. Retail sales didn't interest me or pay well, so I used talents learned as a child making clothes for my dolls to start a custom design shop, designing and making clothes for men and women. Having trouble hiring experienced help, I went to the local college to ask if they would start a class for seamstresses. They asked me to write a course proposal and teach it. I told them I didn't have a teaching degree. The department head said 'Go get one!' I did, and created and taught three courses in commercial sewing and alterations. The students and I operated a 'campus shop' to teach business and alteration skills to them. I taught and trained these students which I could then hire to work in my shop.

For 17 years I ran that business and put up with the increasing jealousy of my husband, who did not want to acknowledge my success nor did he want me to discuss it at all. I sold the business when we divorced. In hindsight, I realize I held onto that business seven years too long, feeling the burn-out we've all experienced at one time after the first ten years of business ownership.

94

My next venture ended after a year and a half, with a knock at my door at 4:00 in the morning. It was the police coming to tell me that my health food store burned in an arson fire. Of course I did not believe the policeman at first and would not even open the door, until I confirmed this was not a prank nor a con man trying to get into my house. Yes, the fire department told me it was true. They asked me where my safe was and I told them I kept money in a cardboard box labeled 'protein powder'. Luckily, after being robbed in the past, I knew enough not to keep much money around. Nevertheless, this was the end of my career as a health food entrepreneur.

This led me into retail. However, after two years of managing ladies' shops in different malls, I realized the corporate mentality and my entrepreneurial mentality were not going to mix. I quit, took off a year, remarried, and planned my goals. Because of the experience I had buying and selling my businesses, I decided to get my real estate license so I could make a living doing it. This was in 1983 and since then I have loved every minute of it.

I specialize in the sale of small businesses in service, retail, distribution and manufacturing. I can represent both sides of the sale and because of my experience, I can be very empathetic; I understand the emotional agony of the seller (having felt it myself), as well as the apprehension and anxiety of the buyer (having felt that also). To close a deal, it must be a win-win situation for both. My job is to control each step, making sure both buyer and seller get a transaction that is fair, honest, ethical, and to the benefit of everyone involved.

Homes are bought on emotion. I have learned that businesses are, too. People dream about owning a business, being their own boss and the success and admiration they will have. But many prospective buyers have little knowledge of the business and lack necessary capital. By being sensitive to emotions at play, by asking open-ended questions, and by using insight, I can usually qualify the buyer and consult them on the decision.

I recently worked with a delightful young woman who was interested in buying a preschool. She had the credentials and experience. After talking for a couple of hours, I discovered her greatest fear: the guilt she would have over losing her husband's money if she failed. I suggested she sit down with her husband and do a 'T' chart -- listing all the concerns and solutions. I also suggested she discuss how her husband felt about her being a success or failure and what his level of support would be. She decided to keep her job.

One of my favorite aspects of the job is investigating the uniqueness of each operation, whether I'm selling it or looking at it for a potential buyer. I get to vicariously run it at no risk! I always find myself daydreaming: How would I manage it? What changes would I make? How would I go about increasing sales? My first listing was a retirement home. When it fell out of escrow, my husband and I bought it.

We've all had our share of funny or memorable business stories. I had one client delay her transaction when her deceased father's body, on route to the Philippines to be buried, got lost. After several failed efforts by the airline, she embarked on a whirlwind search to find the body, flying to Manila, Singapore, and Hong Kong before discovering that his body was in a Tokyo warehouse. I forgave her for the missed appointments.

I also worked with an over anxious client who called for an appraisal of the service business he shared with a partner. Both men were eager to move on. My appraisal came a day late and several dollars short when I presented it to the remaining partner. He had already bought out the other man and paid more than the business was worth.

My husband of ten years is a delightful man and we have a great marriage. He is proud of my business, he supports me in my decisions, and he helps when he can. We both like to travel and garden, and despite his handicap (he had polio as a child and has difficulty walking), we have wonderful times traveling to far places and seeing the beauty of the world. To make sure we get to Hawaii every year we bought a condo there.

Bill is nicknamed 'The Mayor of A Street' because he has lived there, in the same house, for 45 years. Three years ago we reinstigated what had become a forgotten tradition of A Street... block parties. Our third annual, held this year in the middle of the street, was our best yet with music, dancing, a children's bike parade, pinatas, and food, food, food!

During the Persian Gulf War, we sent a letter to 'Any Serviceperson, USA', as encouraged by Dear Abby. I sat down one night and typed out three pages, all about Bill and me, and sent it off. Then I thought, 'Now what 19 or 20 year old is going to respond?' So I sent out 14 more. We were flabbergasted when we received 12 replies! We adopted 11 sons and 1 daughter, writing weekly and sending each one a 20 pound package once a month. Every night for months, after dinner, I baked cookies, which, along with homemade jellies, smoked sausages, and some necessities, we packed in boxes, using peanuts as packing materials. At Christmas time we had a big patio party, invited all our neighbors, and we sat baking and wrapping presents. A little two year old wrapped toothbrushes. We sent 14 boxes filled with artificial trees, Christmas decorations, fruit from our backyards, and homemade goodies. Ours was the only package one dear son received on Christmas Eve. What a thrill we had, going to the airport when the war was over to welcome our first son home! We had a party for each one who came home to Southern California. All of our adopted children are back in the United States, and we have been able to meet seven of our sons and our daughter. We love each one dearly and continue our relationships. In addition to our adopted kids, I have one son, Peter, who at 31 is recently engaged. We are looking forward to (someday) being able to show a picture of a grandchild rather than a granddog.

My advice to a woman entrepreneur is to know yourself and prepare yourself to the best of your ability before going into business. Keep up your knowledge through education, associations, and support groups. Make your own decisions; do not be afraid to recognize your mistakes, be tenacious and flexible. Above all, always keep a positive attitude. Your employees and your clients will appreciate it. Also, remember to have fun! Other than the birth of my sons, being an entrepreneur has been the most exciting and fulfilling experience of my life.

Would I do it all over again? Yes, yes, yes! But perhaps I would not do it the same way. I made my share of mistakes, learned from them and moved on. Some were costly both financially and emotionally. I sought help when I needed it and tried not to dwell on the past. My businesses have given me excitement, joy and satisfaction. I've learned about many lines of work, met wonderful people, and made a lot of friends along the way."

TOLIN BUSINESS APPRAISERS
165 A Street, Tustin, CA 92680
TEL: (714) 832-1630, FAX: (714) 832-1630*

ISABEL B. MEDINA

AOK PROMOTIONS

Isabel (Liz) Medina, president and owner of AOK Promotions in Deer Park, New York, is well-known for her many contributions to the business community, women in business, and the Hispanic community. Liz grew up in Spanish Harlem, worked for an import-export company, married, had children, worked along with her husband to establish a business, and then started her own business. Her business, AOK LTD., was selected in 1983 as one of the top 400 Hispanic businesses. Liz was elected as a delegate to the White House Conference on Small Business in both 1980 and 1986. She was named Minority Business Advocate of the Year 1990, is a member of the Board of Directors of the United State Hispanic Chamber of Commerce and incorporator of the Long Island Hispanic Chamber of Commerce. In 1990 she was chosen as a member of the Bi-County Commission on Peacetime Economics. Liz Medina has dedicated herself to the improvement of the business climate for Hispanics and women. She has looked at the business world as a great and exciting challenge with new horizons to explore and mountains to climb.

"I always think of myself as a business person first, second as a woman, then as a Hispanic.....

Sometimes I wonder 'Whatever possessed me to go into business?' When I graduated from Julia Richman High School in New York City, my first thoughts were of college. At that time I aspired to become a medical doctor. I had good grades, I liked school and at that time being a doctor was the sure way of earning good money and being respected by all. My parents who were not college graduates or professionals encouraged me. I entered New York University and it didn't take me too long to realize that scholastics, especially the sciences, weren't really what I wanted. The challenge was exhilarating but the work was tedious. I have always liked to interact with people and hitting the books wasn't doing it for me.

After three years at New York University, I left thinking at the time, to take a six month break and come back the next semester. I needed time to sort things out. Not having a family that had been college educated made it tough to make some decisions. This was my first exposure to having to make decisions by myself that would affect the rest of my life.

I left school and got a job in an import-export company. I had no office skills, but soon realized how invaluable my speaking, reading and writing Spanish was. I recall, as a child, how I rebelled when Mom insisted that we all sit at the kitchen table for an hour as she tutored us in Spanish. I hated it then because all the other children were out playing and here I was studying again after a full school day. I later appreciated the time taken out for these lessons. Mom's ideas were, that we had to learn English in school, but that we would never forget our Hispanic roots, culture or language.

I was a quick study and I learned quickly on the job. I do believe that having been disciplined at home, to take time out to sort things and put them in proper perspective, became an asset in the workplace. I had to learn the skills needed for different positions that I wanted and 'go for it'. I was rapidly promoted. I have never forgotten this lesson. In Spanish we say, 'el querer es poder', loosely translated this means if you want something badly enough you can get it.

Along the way, I met the man who was to be my future husband and thoughts of returning to school faded. I married, moved to suburbia, had two children, helped my husband establish a business, worked along with him in the business and soon realized just how much I loved it. I had found my niche in life. The going was very tough. Money was scarce and we started in the basement of our house. At night after my husband came home from work, his job that he still held, we put the children to bed and started working on the one contract we had. We were into brazing and welding of metal parts and I soon learned all about this job too. In the mornings I was a familiar sight delivering the work to our customers, towing the two children along with me. I never thought of this as hard work. As the children grew, I continued to work at the business, did PTA, Little League, Cub Scouts and all sort of community activities.

When my husband went into another field, I went along with him. By this time we had a small factory, employees and all the problems that go along with this success. Again this to me was another learning experience. When I decided to go out on my own, after my husband went into a different field, my husband was my staunchest supporter. He never let me believe that because I was a woman I could not achieve in business. As a Hispanic and a woman, I very soon came to see that there existed all sorts of stereotypes out in the business world. I also learned that government and big business considered me a minority. I had never been accorded this designation before and it was a surprise to say the least.

Naivete has its drawbacks but I found a way to use it to my advantage. If I behaved simply as a business person, people had no choice but to treat me as such. I found out that there were contracts that I could bid on because of this designation and I used this for my own enrichment in business. As a minority I was supposed to have been poor and deprived and neglected. If I had been all of this I certainly didn't feel it. I look back on my childhood days in Spanish Harlem as a plus. Certainly the

Spanish Harlem of today is not that of the one of my era, but as I look back I feel that I was very rich; rich in love, family friends and culture. Perhaps these are the things that are essential to keep you going forward, they were to me.

I have been in all different fields of business. I have been in manufacturing, foods and promotional items yet I have found them all to be essentially the same. It means that you work without looking at a time clock, learning to market your company and/or its products or skills, it means learning to talk to your accountant intelligently, reading your own P&L statement and finding out that although your employees get paid every week, you may not get a paycheck. All these lessons just mean that as a business owner, you work harder, longer, perhaps get paid less and only you can pat yourself on the back when something goes very well. It is primarily learning to believe in yourself and that you can 'DO'.

I had my greatest success when I owned a metal fabrication factory. We did machining, welding and brazing here. I was in a non-traditional field for a woman and I did receive some flack. However, behaving as a lady, but one that knew what she was talking about, won me many friends in this arena. After proving myself, competitively, pricewise and quality wise, I was treated as one of the 'boys'. At this point in my business life I negotiated one of the biggest contracts of my life. I won the bid competitively from the government, was the low bidder and then was rejected. I learned to put my fighting gloves on then. I called my attorney, fought for the contract and won. At this same time I was elected as a delegate to the White House Conference on Small Business.

This was my training ground for getting involved on a national level for Hispanics and women business owners. At the time that I completed this major contract I realized that these jobs were drying up. Large corporations were bidding for the same jobs I was and I could not compete pricewise against them. Lesson learned--when you realize that the monies and contracts are not coming in, cut back on everything, cut your losses and look for new sources of revenue. Never be afraid to be creative. I have also learned that the revenues you will receive from one

102

source should never be more than fifty percent of your income.

I decided to close down this operation and give myself full time to serving on various committees to try to help and improve the business climate for Hispanics and women. Remember I wear two hats; I am Hispanic and a woman. As a business person I always think of myself as a business person first, second as a woman, and third as a Hispanic. When you do this you look at things through three different perspectives. All of which are very important, because you are using skills acquired over the years. All those organizational skills that used to run a home, PTA meetings, church raffles, Little League, etc. are of utmost importance, slightly different connotations but very nearly alike. These areas have been my schoolroom for a degree in business. You are constantly learning from people around you who would never consider themselves teachers.

In 1986 I was again elected to the White House Conference on Small Business. Again, it was a wonderful learning experience. There were also disappointments, one of the greatest was the support of the delegates across the nation for the 'English Only' bill. We should realize that as the world becomes smaller, the learning of foreign languages will become crucial as an essential business tool. How can we talk about international sales unless we learn the languages and cultures of the world that surrounds us?

Because I think of myself as a business person, not just a business woman, I believe that this is why I have accomplished so many things and earned the respect of so many people. When my business AOK was selected in 1983 as one of the top 400 Hispanic businesses in 1983 I was on top of the world. When I was awarded the Minority Business Advocate of the Year, 1990, for my region, I was again elated - another goal reached. In 1990 I was elected to the Board of Directors of the United States Hispanic Chamber of Commerce. That was the highlight of my career. When two male friends and I incorporated the Long Island Hispanic Chamber of Commerce three years ago, I had reached yet another goal. I was chosen as a member of the Bi-County Commission on Peacetime

Economics in 1990 and appointed to the Hispanic Advisory Board of Suffolk County. None of these are paying positions. I balance these jobs with my business and my personal life. I have found that if you are in business you must be aware of the political, civic and business scenario. Legislative issues have a way of impacting on business, especially on small business, on your community, your geographical area nationally and most especially on your ethnicity. We owe it to ourselves to be diversified and be committed to these endeavors. This is the sign of a committed business person. When you think of resting on your laurels, think again, for if you are to be truly successful you must be committed.

As individuals we are comprised of components which make up the many layers that we are. I have used my education, my culture, my ethnicity and my femininity to enhance my walk through the business world. I have never forgotten that whatever I take out I must replenish. What were my weaknesses became my strengths and that is how I look at the business world; a great challenge and always new horizons to explore and many mountains to climb. But, I have never forgotten to give back to my community, or to my fellow business people."

AOK PROMOTIONS
90 Jefryn Boulevard, Deer Park, New York 11729
TEL: (516) 242-1642, FAX: (516) 643-1332

DAWN WELLS

WISHING WELLS COLLECTIONS

Dawn Wells, a 4th generation Nevadan, was a chemistry major at Stephens College, graduated from the University of Washington with a degree in theatre, was named Miss Nevada, and then spent three years playing the television role of Mary Ann on "Gilligan's Island". Each year, Dawn hosts and co-produces The Children's Miracle Network Telethon. Her associations with and concern for the physically challenged and her experience with the theatre and quick change costuming resulted in her business, Wishing Wells Collections, a manufacturer of easy-to-put-on and colorful clothing for the physically challenged. Dawn also has a business with Marcia Wallace. Wallace & Wells Workshops offers seminars on self esteem and how to market yourself in the acting place. Dawn served on the Board of Curators at Stephens College and sometimes teaches advanced acting there. She has received the Alumnae Achievement Award, been commencement speaker and was awarded the Alpha Chi Omega Outstanding Civic Leadership Award 1990 and the Case Award for Volunteer of the Year for Colleges and Universities. She is a board member of The Sycamores, a residential facility for disturbed and abused boys. *Editor's Note:* We heard a rumor that a musical version of "Gilligan's Island" is in the works and Dawn and 'The Professor' may be playing Mr. and Mrs. Howell.

"Plan like you are going to live forever and live like you are going to die tomorrow...

I was born and raised in Reno, a 4th generation Nevadan. I think some of the tenacity a person acquires is from overcoming certain obstacles. I didn't have anything really major, but I came from a divorced home which I consider an advantage because I felt like I had two families. I was influenced very strongly by my father and my mother and my grandmother, all positive thinkers about work principles, ethics and the philosophy that you're rewarded if you do the job well. I was pretty active in school...good grades, honor roll, student activities. I didn't do any acting at all in high school. I auditioned and never got a part but I was a public speaker, Girl's Stater and debater, valedictorian and that sort of thing. I was well-rounded I suppose you would say. I had aspirations of becoming a ballerina. That's what I wanted to do more than anything. I took 12 years of ballet but developed trick knees and had to give up dance and all sports. I spent most of my time in high school in a cast from my ankle to my hip on one leg or the other because my knees dislocated.

I had the wonderful opportunity of going to Stephens College, an all women's college. Along with the influence of my family, I think Stephens really provided me with a sense of self. I was a chemistry major but, because of my inability to participate in any physical education, I was encouraged to take theatre courses as my outlet. I really fell in love with it and I guess I was pretty good. Stephens was a two-year women's college and I had to go somewhere else for my junior and senior year. My advisor talked me into changing my major to theatre and I selected the University of Washington in Seattle where I graduated with honors.

About that time I was asked to run for Miss Nevada. I thought it was ridiculous! I just couldn't do it. Then the more I thought about it, and since acting was my main goal, I knew that it would be good experience to get up in front of that large an audience. I had no concept that I would win but thought it would be a great challenge to see if I could do something like that in front of so many people. To my great surprise I did win and then participated in the Miss America Pageant, another very worthwhile experience.

At graduation time I needed to make a decision as to where I should go. An aspiring actress could only make a living in New

106

York or Los Angeles. I did not want to be collecting unemployment and saying, 'I'm an actress.' I gave myself a year and said that if I didn't accomplish my goal, I would probably go back to school to be either a pediatrician or a lawyer. New York was musical comedy and I couldn't sing, so I chose to come to Los Angeles but had no fantasy of becoming a movie star. If I could support myself and work that's what I would do. I graduated from college and while making the transition visited my father on the Idaho side of the Teton Mountains. A friend of my friend was doing the melodrama in Jackson Hole, Wyoming, and I had driven over to that side of the mountain to see his performance. The director and producer had a fight and the director was fired. His wife was the leading lady so I stepped in the next night with a book in my hand and finished the run. This was my first professional job. I got $14.00 a week and we all had to clean the theatre. When I finished in Jackson Hole I came to Los Angeles. I went to see several agents and got the second thing I auditioned for. I think part of it was the experience of my training.

I think Stephens College was also a part of it. University of Washington was a wonderful theatre school, too, but Stephens has a way of bringing out the sense of self and what you are about...what you are best at, chemistry, riding horses or whatever. I think a women's college is a real advantage because you have the opportunity of developing as a leader without becoming too aggressive and without having to compete with men. You graduate knowing who you are and it's done with femininity. I can't explain it but there is a feminine strength in a lot of the women that come out of the school. In my first class reunion at Stephens College we had a woman who with her husband and five children had built their house by hand brick by brick. We had a woman who came in second in a race for Mayor of Houston. We had the voice of the first Houston Astros female sportscaster and a woman who is now writing for Sesame Street. There was also a woman who was in charge of all of the education coming into the United Nations.

In Los Angeles I was very lucky. I worked right away and soon went into Gilligan's Island as Mary Ann, which I feel was probably a turning point in my life. One of the things my father used to say to me was **'Plan like you are going to live forever and live like you are going to die tomorrow.'** There is something about coming down a path. If you are prepared, you can accomplish something at any crossroad. It's the luck of the draw whether you pick left or right. But if you are trained and ready when you have that opportunity fall at your feet, you have a chance to do something about it. You may only get two or three times in your life where opportunity or luck happens. If you have the courage and the training to go with it, it will make a difference.

I think I got Gilligan's Island because of my experience, not so much the years, but where I had come from...what roads I had taken. It was one of those opportunities in my life when I took the ball and went with it so to speak. After my run as Mary Ann on Gilligan's Island, I was afraid that if I stayed in Los Angeles, I would become type-cast. So I used the opportunity of the name value and the semi celebrity status that Mary Ann achieved to go out and grow in my craft. I did theatre across the country and I got cast in roles in which I might not have been cast in film. It was a risk, I might have walked into another series and gotten a million dollars, but as an actress I didn't feel that I would have grown. I spent a great deal of time making that growth process.

I feel like certain things offer you challenges. One of them for me was to do a musical since I didn't sing. At age 40 I had that opportunity. I trained a very long time and did it. One of the things I say when I do guest speaking is that doing that musical gave me satisfaction of trying for the impossible. I wasn't great, but I was adequate. Some of the time I wasn't very good and I was never wonderful. But it was a dream that I fulfilled. Just taking a step toward an unreachable goal is something you need to try in your lifetime. If you want to be a jet pilot or the president of a company, you have to set that goal or you won't reach any other level. You have to learn where you are to take the next step. Doing *They're Playing Our Song* gave me some ideas for starting my business, **Wishing Wells Collections.**

Because my grandmother was a stroke victim and my mother took care of her, I learned at a very young age what it was like to take care of someone who was incapacitated. Also the man with whom I was in love for a number of years had his mother in a nursing home. Every time I visited her, the only people that appeared to have any sense of dignity or self worth, were the people who had daughters who could sew and put together a fairly attractive outfit. One day when I was out on tour with 'They're Playing Our Song', we had all of those 30-second velcro down the back costume changes. I thought there must be some way of creating something for people who are infirm or recovering, to provide them with a sense of well being and to help them feel better about themselves...a sense of healing and all those things that physical, positive images do for us. The University of Pennsylvania is doing a study on make-up for covering radiation scarring and how it helps the healing process by making the person feel better about herself. The minute you are ill and infirm and put into that situation, your identity and individuality are taken away. It is almost like a penal institution...as if they put a number on that hospital gown and you no longer have your identity. I decided there must be a way of developing a line of clothing in nice colorful fabrics, industrially washable and easy to put on. I hoped to make a difference in the patients' lives and also in the caregivers' who have to lift people who are incapable of dressing themselves.

I also host and co-produce the Children's Miracle Network Telethon for the State of Missouri. This is also one of the reasons I conceived the idea for the clothes. I had a very young wonderful cystic fibrosis lady that I met and knew for about six years. She underwent a heart and lung transplant at Stanford University. I spent every weekend with her for 187 days. She was always asking me if she couldn't have something in color to wear. I was giving her garments. She would sleep in them and try them and then give me input. We lost her but she changed my life. She taught me to see the need for spirit and color. She was not elderly and it was a temporary time for her, but she felt the need for something to brighten her life.

My cousin, Terry Lee Wells, from Reno, helped me some as I began with my original concept. Terry made the story boards and thought of the idea of putting colored swatches around in a wheel. The color wheel was of different fabrics. One would be the color of the bathrobe and others would be all the nightshirts that would go with it. We really got into the spirit. We cut up samples for about a year before I branched out and started the process of beginning the business of Wishing Wells Collections. Stephens College has a fabulous fashion department and they showed me how to present ideas on a board and incorporate the fabrics. A young woman pattern maker here helped me with the design for the first nightgown with color and quality. I researched the business and learned how to develop a sample line. Janice Olson, a young girl who was also a Stephens graduate designed our first catalog and helped me with the name and my logo. The fabric houses would not give us the time of day because we were not ordering more than 500 yards of a particular fabric. It was a problem getting patterns from the pattern maker to the sample maker to the manufacturer. I couldn't find anybody who was interested in making a small number of garments. I think what really won out in the end was persistence. Finally one big fabric company said that they would see if they could find 500 yards of something that no one else was going to take. We worked very hard. I remember when the PR people wanted a shot of me with all the fabric bolts, we got garbage cans and dollies and went downtown in Los Angeles where people were sleeping in the streets and rolled our fabrics from Point A to Point B. We developed a sample line and went around trying to get it produced and actually found a little manufacturer, a cutter, a sewer and a distributor and produced our first line. I had to make a commitment and manufacture 'X-amount' before I put our first catalog out. We might eat half of those garments but had to make enough to get off the ground. We produced our own catalog and began marketing. Terry Lee was only able to help for a little while because of the distance involved between her home in Reno and the business here. Janice was living with me and we worked out of my house until we couldn't stand all the sample garments and the 24-hour days. We'd pass in the hall at 2:00 in the morning saying, 'What do you think about gray flannel?' and talk for a half hour. We were that way for almost two years. That requires a tremendous amount of energy. I had to put my acting role aside and risk turning down opportunities in order to put this business together. I now have a wonderful woman in my office, vice president of marketing and operations. Shana Yao takes the everyday things off my hands. I still have to do much of it myself, like the sales and calling on potential clients, because nobody knows your product as well as you know it yourself.

My role as Mary Ann on Gilligan's Island was great for publicity purposes. Last month in Glamour Magazine Mary Ann was compared to Ginger and the article talked about the attainability of Mary Ann. She was the one you could bring home to your mother and ask to the prom. Gilligan's Island is the longest running show in the history of television. I just did a particular commercial and the producer said that the reason I was picked was because his mother knew who I was, he knew who I was and his children knew who I was. In the Solomon Islands, in the middle of the Pacific Ocean, where there was no electricity and no running water and I had come to the island by canoe, the chief's wife said, 'I know you.' I got on an airplane coming out of Disneyworld a couple of years ago and the whole plane started singing the Gilligan song. Mary Ann was a sweet and likeable character. It was a help to my business. Newspapers and radio stations would talk to me because of Mary Ann. I would say that 50% of the letters coming in to me said something like, 'Oh, I knew Mary Ann would think of something nice like this to do.' Everyone was very positive about our clothing. The product is great. It's the marketing that is very tough...trying to find the care giver. How do I know that it's your mother that is ill? There has been a very high response rate from the PR that I have done and from catalogs that have been sent out. Buying good mailing lists from other catalog companies and sending them to nursing homes or sending them to rehab has been very difficult. It is very interesting trying to penetrate the nursing home market. My pet peeve is that if you are in a nursing home, that is usually where you will spend the rest of your life. It isn't a question of needing a nightgown. You need a dress! You need some garment to wear that makes you a person. You are not an invalid in bed. It is your residence.

So I think part of my goal is to try to do some lobbying to see if we can change some minds. By the year 2000 every 5th American will be over the age of 65. We are going to have to deal with this issue at some point. I have a meeting coming up shortly with a nursing home chain and I have made contact with the Visiting Nurses' Association. 80% of the elderly are being taken care of at home. I feel that if I will continue to improve design and keep the doors open, we will eventually reach the marketplace. Everybody knows the need is there. It is just a question of marketing.

Recently I took a time management course because I have such a variety of things going on in my life. There may be a musical of Gilligan's Island and the 'Professor' and I may play Mr. and Mrs. Howell. Marcia Wallace and I have Wallace & Wells Workshops. We give seminars on self esteem and how to market yourself in the acting place. In addition to the Telethon, I have just been named spokesperson for the new Children's Center at the University of Missouri Hospital in Columbia. I also served on the Board of Curators at Stephens College and served as chairman of the development board on the Board of Curators. I am very active with the school and am on campus three or four times a year. I teach advanced acting at Stephens when I can. I am going to do a play there in October and I do a lot of personal consultations with the students on marketing yourself to go out into the theatrical world. I try to say to those I'm teaching that having training and talent does not mean that you will work. You have to combine the art form with business. If you want to earn a living and be successful at acting, you have to market it. Sometimes you come into yourself at 35 as a character actress who wouldn't make it at 20. The real advantage, and one that I wish I could have had, is to have someone who will tell you the truth. 'You have a great voice and should be trying voice overs.' 'Maybe you should think about waiting to become a character actress.' 'Maybe you just aren't good enough in this area, but perhaps you should be a wardrobe person, or a makeup person, or a prop person, or work in some area of the business that you love and would be good at. The theatrical world requires great perseverance. I feel that if you can discourage a would be actor or actress, they haven't got enough of what it takes. I try to talk them out of it and see who says, 'I don't care what you say. I'm going to do it anyway.'

I believe that when you reach a certain stage in your life you have to give something back. I have a very hard time when people say that a child has no hope. You look at some of the areas in downtown Los Angeles where three and four families live in one apartment. The parents don't even know where the kids are going to school. The kids don't have a chance to make it unless they excel in sports or are really talented in some area that gives them a sense of self worth at a young age. I feel very fortunate that I have been successful. It has been hard work, but also luck to be in the right place when things happen. If you get to that point, it is important to share.

One of the hardest things to do is to know when to let go. I never learned to and I tend to stick to a thing until it's dead. I think I must have a western heritage or pioneer spirit. There really are differences in women from the south, the north, the midwest and the west. I think that pioneer spirit probably comes from being raised in Nevada. Part of my courage comes from the fact that I have always managed my own money and my own business, which is very difficult in the entertainment field because it is so uncertain. You may make a lot of money one year and then you may not work for two. You have to have courage and belief. I think that helped me in the business world.

I believe a woman can do anything she sets her mind to. I believe anybody can...male or female. We women are so much more capable than we even realize. I feel that you should always follow your dream and not let anybody discourage or dissuade you. You will never know if you can do something until you try."

MARIE REIKO MIYASHIRO, APR
MARIE REIKO PUBLIC RELATIONS

Marie Reiko Miyashiro started Marie Reiko Public Relations (MRPR), a three person, Honolulu-based firm in 1985. She was 24 years old, had less than a year's experience in public relations and had little money, but she had other strengths that were essential. MRPR is one of the fastest growing independent public relations agencies in Hawaii. She is a lecturer in the University of Hawaii's communications department and a frequent speaker to business associations and women's groups conferences. Qualities like the ability to visualize success, energy and a willingness to change and grow led her agency to pick up well known local, national and international clients. Marie was earning six figures before she was 30 and had pared her work week down to four days. Born and raised in Hawaii, she lives in Honolulu and surfs, writes and sings for relaxation.

113

"I can usually tell what kind of day it will be within the first few minutes that I walk into my office.....

Early on in my self-employed career, it became obvious that for the entrepreneur, the work day often begins when your eyes open in the morning. You are still in bed and already have a to-do list several pages thick.

When I speak or am interviewed for small business articles, people ask, 'What is your typical day like?' While there really isn't any typical day, the following story does illustrate a number of techniques I use during my work day as well as some insight into how closely work and home life are related.

I know as soon as I wake up this morning that I am late. It is already 6:45 a.m. Traffic will be bad. I'd be lucky if I could get into the office by 7:30. There are three files, five memos and six E-mails waiting for me. The Staff comes in at 8:00 a.m. Then there's Dallas/Fort Worth. I always call beyond the West Coast before 8:00 a.m. for the rates and to catch my clients before lunch.

Lunch. Who am I having lunch with today? Where? Should I wear my comfortable flat patent leather Ferragamo shoes, or the 'make-me-look-taller' high heels? The black electronic organizer scrolls through today's appointments. What a relief. No lunch scheduled. '9:00 a.m. Lori,' it reads.

I do not believe in ironing. It takes too long, no one ever notices anyway, and Astrid does it every other Wednesday. Today, like any day, I pull on whatever is ready-to-go and comfortable. Comfort at the office does not have to be sacrificed for tailored good looks. Mostly, I wear fashionable slacks and a jacket. All my clothes are made of natural fibers, cottons and wools, autumn colors. I have only one pair of high-heeled shoes because I can keep my nearly running walking pace better in low heels. I wear knee-high 'old lady' nylons or socks. One of my partners, Louise Saffery, has said, 'How would men like it if they had to wrap Saran Wrap around their legs all day and walk around on a pair of stilts?' It took me

114

three years to be willing to wear what I consider comfortable. That was two years ago.

As I hurry to get dressed, I practice ten ways to say no. No raise for Lori. She's going to ask for one again. It's no. It's not that she doesn't deserve a raise, it's just that Lori's had a few false starts in this new position.

I hop on one foot while slipping a sock onto the other. Okay, I look down at my feet and wiggle my toes. Socks and toes, ready to go. Lori will have her raise in three months.

Since Labor Day, 1990, my Monday-Friday morning ritual, the same routine I had repeated like clockwork for six years, has taken a decidedly softer approach, namely in the form of one calico cat. The first pet that I have ever owned, I took one look at those tiny paws and trusting eyes and named her 'Sweetie.' After two nights at home chasing the little one out from under everything, the six-week-old kitten was renamed 'Scooters'. Scooters is the morning wake-up call in this household. The condo cat, she is compact and cleeeeeeean, jumps on the bed and kneads my stomach like clockwork at 6:00 a.m. On weekends, we both sleep in. No work morning begins without the ritual 'cat toss'. This is a procedure involving the exiting through the front door by the human species only and the feline species remaining in the condominium. The right hand holds the cat inside while the left had holds the doorknob from the outside. With one motion, Scooters is sent flying three feet away, legs spread eagle. This gives my left hand time to shut the door without the cat being outside -- bad -- or in between the door and the door jam -- worse. My friends think it is funny. But for me and Scooters, it's just the new morning routine.

Pets, I am told, love unconditionally. Huh? Scooters would do well in the world of business, ignoring all the regulating conditions, always conditional. You do this, and then...I'll do that. If. Then. Not bad. Not good. Just the way it is.

If it's before 8:30 a.m., the black Saab heads into downtown along Beretania Street. If it's after 8:30 a.m., it's on to the freeway and off at Vineyard Boulevard to get to Punchbowl Street, then Beretania and finally Richards, the entrance to the parking garage. The magnetic key card slides through the slot, the light turns from red to green and the wooden entry arm raises to salute me through. If it's before 8:30 a.m., it's the orange or green floor. If it's after 8:30 a.m., it's the top purple floor, eleven or twelve treacherous parking garage corners later.

On some mornings, when business is thin and bills are thick or when one of my employees has accused me of some mortal sin, the one flight of winding stairs to my second floor office, seems like an endless maze. On other mornings, I fly up skipping steps humming to myself. The double entry doors welcome me into the lobby. I get to my office, switch on the Macintosh. Hum. Zing. Ding. It logs on. Sitting in my high back chair, I pull the hands-free telephone headset on and tuck the mouthpiece up and away until the day's first call, flip open the Sharp electronic organizer. It's a calendar; no, it's an alarm; no it's a rolodex---all in one!

7:45 a.m. I fill my mug at the purified water dispenser. I'm ready for...The Staff. I will spend three hours in meetings with them, another couple hours on the telephone -- mostly leaving messages -- an hour editing or reviewing documents, and an hour -- a very important hour -- working on something which does not have to be done today. This is my '10% rule'. I am fiendish about spending at least 10 percent of my day planning, developing, making concrete a future, non-urgent project.

This is creative time. I relax into an idea and put it to paper or computer screen. Big pictures bubble up before me, sounds smell of the future. I am a time traveller to the tomorrow. Over and over, different scenes play in full Technicolor and I dream up solutions of how to get from there to here. Backwards planning. From there to here, not here to there. Sometimes, I forget to eat. To an onlooker, I appear catatonic.

Lately, I have spent my 10% time working not on accounts, but on profit-sharing plans, employee medical benefits packages, staffing requests and soliciting and listening to the concerns and goals of the two key account staff.

116

It's a nasty job but someone has to be president. And since I have the title and own Marie Reiko Public Relations, I am it. The transition from sole worker bee to manager and now, president is a curious one for me. Essentially, I woke up one day and realized I had a new job. That if I took care of the accounts and the account staff took care of the accounts, too, they would forever be in conflict. I had to give up doing their job and make my job instead, the taking care of staff, servicing them first and the clients second. It goes against everything I've learned in six years. The minute I hired a good account staff, I went from being the aggressive, bread-winner, out-there-with-the clients 'father', to the nurturing, patient, in-here-with-the-troops 'mother'.

I can usually tell what kind of day it will be in the first few minutes I walk into the office. How? Because my day has little to do with events or others, it has mostly to do with my frame of mind. If I meditated in the morning, got a good night's sleep, had some vigorous and enjoyable exercise in the last 24 hours, odds are good it will be a good day. My body is the most expensive piece of equipment my company owns.

If my work is a struggle, and some days it is, I take time out and go for a walk. If my day is awful, I leave for the beach. On days where leaving is not possible, I go right into my heart. What kinds of feelings am I trying to avoid? What is making my life so hard at this moment? What do I need to do to take care of my own emotional discomfort right now so that I can give of myself in my work?

Sure, anybody can 'do what they love' as the old saying goes. But success also is learning hundreds of techniques to love what you do and love yourself while doing it over and over again. Because in a small business, it is not 'If something bad happens, what will I do?', it is, 'When something bad happens, what will I do?'

Here I am at my desk wondering what the day will bring. The secret to running any business is all in the mind. The secret to remaining successful at it is all in the heart. Success as a small business owner is made up of much more than just the nuts and bolts of running a business. If it is true that nine out of ten businesses will close before their fifth year, but once they reach that point they tend to be long lived, then more than half of making it as an entrepreneur is setting your life up to support your business for the first five years. Your home life, having a pet, getting a good night's sleep, allowing ample creative time in the office, a regular exercise program and being willing to take time out during the day, are all very important ingredients to entrepreneurial success."

MARIE REIKO PUBLIC RELATIONS
Queen's Plaza, Suite 212,
801 Alakea Street, Honolulu, Hawaii 96813
TEL: (808) 599-4242, FAX: (808) 599-5885

GERRY VOGT

MRS. GERRY'S KITCHEN, INC.

Gerry Vogt was born and raised in Minnesota. After her graduation in 1963 from Albert Lea High School, she worked in various capacities including a bank for two and a half years and then took a job as head cashier and bookkeeper in a local grocery store. She married her husband, Jerry Vogt, in 1967 and has three grown children. She is founder and President of Mrs. Gerry's Kitchen, Inc., headquartered in Albert Lea, a town of 20,000 in Southern Minnesota. Mrs. Gerry's Kitchen has grown from a small commercial building with a small cooler, two stoves, and a sink to a completely modern facility containing 39,000 square feet and "state of the art" machinery. In 1973 she started making salads as an addition to the meat products distributed by her husband. Using recipes from her own kitchen and with her parents as her first two employees, they produced 70,000 pounds of salad. In 1990, the company produced over eleven and a half million pounds of salad. Their products now include potato salad, macaroni salad, and coleslaw plus 80 other salads, a dessert line, spreads, dips for fruits and vegetables and a full line of gelatin products.

119

"In the beginning men did not take me seriously.....

The beginning of Mrs. Gerry's was an idea, a dream. In spite of the problems encountered by a woman running a corporation with growing pains, I turned it into a successful corporation with midwest distribution of a quality product. Today, Mrs. Gerry's Kitchen is one of Albert Lea's and Minnesota's distinguished corporations. It is a well-known, well-run industry.

I made my dream a reality with hard work, determination, innovation, great skills, faith in God, moral support from my husband, and encouragement plus cooperation from Albert Lea officials.

In 1963 I graduated from Albert Lea High School. I did not go on to college but my jobs during and after high school helped me in my business. Working in a grocery store as a clerk and then for a bank led to the position of bookkeeper and head cashier of the newest and largest grocery store in Albert Lea. My responsibilities were training of personnel on cash registers, scheduling, managing 55 cashiers and grocery carriers, as well as all office duties which included keeping the books for the store. I believe my lack of formal training on how to run a business was one of my weakest points. I attended business seminars and read all I could to overcome those areas where I needed help.

To best realize the accomplishments of my efforts, it is important to understand the small beginnings of Mrs. Gerry's Kitchen, Inc. The seed was planted for Mrs. Gerry's in 1973 when my husband, Jerry, who is owner of Vogt Distributing, asked me if I would consider making salads as a compliment to his meat products. I agreed, even though I had three small children age six and under at home.

I bought a small 1100 square foot commercial building in Albert Lea. It was remodeled, a cooler built, two stoves and a commercial sink were installed. Our first day of production was December 4, 1973. My first two employees were my parents.

The following spring I hired my sister as my production manager and right hand gal. Over the next five years, the business grew substantially. Plans were developed in 1978 for a new manufacturing plant. Our new plant with 8,000 square feet of space was completed in 1979. Since that time I have found it necessary to increase the size of my plant three times due to an ever increasing demand for the product. New additions were added in 1983, 1985 and 1990 increasing my facility to 39,000 square feet.

I have been in business for 17 years and my special skills are in foods. For the first 12 years, the recipes were mine. I credit my mother for her experience and training in food, but the quality of the product is of the utmost importance to me. My dedication to quality control and a willingness to be innovative and cooperative, along with encouragement from city officials of Albert Lea, have contributed to my success. I demand excellence and quality from my employees.

Of course, as the business and building grew, so did the number of employees. In the beginning, I virtually did every aspect of my business. I was in production, bookkeeping, sales, shipping, buying -- you name it, I did it. With the growth of the business, I hired a secretary and a salesman six years after I started the company.

Knowing when to hire people to help me is one of the keys to my success. The Plant Engineer/Traffic Controller started at age 16 as one of the cleanup crew and advanced to his present position. The Production Manager, hired as a laborer ten years ago, learned her job through on-the-job training and by attending seminars. A Food Technologist with a degree in Food Science is responsible for research, development and quality control. The Vice President of Operations gained his experience in the potato chip industry. In addition, my employees today include ten salespeople, one sales and marketing director who works a fourteen state area, as well as seven secretaries in various capacities in the corporate office. Employment exceeds 100 employees during peak periods. I believe in open communication with all employees. I know most of them by first name and strive to treat them as individuals.

The amount of products sold has increased from 70,000 pounds in the first full year of business to over 11 million pounds in the fiscal year 1990. One of my main problems has been the continuing growth of the company with its almost continual need for additional space. I have directed the company through these changes, working with contractors in design of machinery and workflow through the plant. In addition, I have always worked with financial institutions in the financing of these necessary expansions.

Starting a new company means taking many kinds of risks. Borrowing money to build a manufacturing plant meant risking my own livelihood by personally signing loans for large amounts of money. This risk continues year after year, not only on loans, but with the success and profitability of the company. Many families (employees) depend on the success of this company for their livelihood. I take that responsibility very seriously.

In 1975, four additional distributors added Mrs. Gerry's salads to their product lines. When 15 additional distributors were added the following year and the company began supplying new accounts to retail warehouses and food service warehouses, a new location was needed. I developed a comphehensive business plan and worked through that plan very carefully. I followed it and lead my company through all the changes necessary to expand and grow while still maintaining excellence. It has always been my philosophy to produce the best possible product and to make this philosophy work with the help of loyal and long time employees.

In a 17 year period, under my direction and leadership, a homegrown manufacturing plant evolved into a community leader and regional supplier of salads, desserts, fruit and vegetable dips, vegetable spreads, and a full line of gelatin products. From 1984 through 1990, our sales growth increases were 80%, 41%, 20%, 11%, 11%, and 16% respectively. These increases were due in part to our country's dependence on convenience foods and I feel because of the high quality products produced by Mrs. Gerry's. Our salads are made with no preservatives, artificial colorings or flavoring. My commitment and dedication to high quality has kept our products tasting as if they were made in your own kitchen.

Over the years as my company was growing, I was faced with many problems and was forced to find a solution. Being a woman in the manufacturing business is probably the greatest adversity I have had to overcome. I encountered some employees, salesmen, and contractors in the development and expansion of the plant who refused to work for or with a woman.

My credibility has been doubted by many individuals who have found it hard to accept the fact that I am the president of this successful corporation and I am the one who 'calls the shots'. I have overcome these adversities strictly through my own determination to be accepted and recognized as a leader of a growing company.

One of the hardest problems was dealing with the fact of having three small children at home when I had huge responsibilities in my business. My loving husband helped me the most in solving that problem. During the day I had a very reliable 75 year old woman come to my home to care for the children. She was wonderful! She took care of them and loved them as though they were her own grandchildren. After my husband was finished with his work for the day, he went home to the children. He cooked for them, played with them, bathed them, and tucked them in when I wasn't home. Without him, I know I couldn't have done it. He was great!

I have and still do enjoy my company very much, particularly the relationship I have with my employees. They are like a second family. They are a wonderful group of people. We all work hard together as a team and also enjoy each other's company when it comes time to have fun at parties, picnics, golf outings, or just a chat over coffee in the lunch room.

My advice to other entrepreneurs is to set high goals and work hard to reach those goals. Keep your hands in the business and don't expect others to do the work. I feel the reason for the success of Mrs. Gerry's is that I, the owner, work the business everyday. When someone with a personal interest in the business oversees daily activity, there is less chance of the business failing. Also, I asked our Lord to give me the strength and knowledge to run this business, and I know He is beside me every day."

MRS. GERRY'S KITCHEN, INC.
2110 Y.H. Hanson Ave.
P. O. Box 1127, Albert Lea, MN 56007
TEL: (507) 373-6384, FAX: (507) 373-5617

BETTYE L. SMITH
ALASKA BUSINESS COLLEGE

Bettye L. Smith captivates the vitality of Alaska. A pioneer and Alaskan leader, she built successful businesses in the male dominated northern frontier of forty years ago. Mrs. Smith's achievements included founding Alaska Business College 35 years ago, advertising specialty sales, employment agencies, temporary help services and other diverse firms. She has served on both national, state and local boards and commissions as well as dedicating time to civic organizations and promoting quality local, state, national and international vocational education. (Editor's Note: Bettye started her business career in Fairbanks by teaching typing in her kitchen and advanced dictation in a converted bedroom. In 1985 she moved to Anchorage, borrowed money, and with sheer determination to succeed, opened Alaska Business College. In 1989 Phillips Colleges bought her out and it became Alaska Jr. College. On May 16, 1991, the college dedicated the Alaska Jr. College Bettye L. Smith Resource Learning Library in her name.)

"Today I believe a woman can do and be anything she wants to be and do.....

In 1955, when my second daughter was born, I wanted to stay home with my two daughters, but we needed money. I had attended business college and worked as a secretary for many years, so I decided that I could teach secretarial subjects in my home. Working outside the home had created friction in the marriage so thought that might make things better.

Prior to making this decision, due to a difficult pregnancy, I had returned to Idaho to stay with my family and be closer to the medical services that I needed. During the pregnancy, to keep busy, I attended Nampa Business College in Nampa, Idaho. There I was introduced to Speedwriting Shorthand, found out no one had the franchise in Alaska, made arrangements for the franchise, returned to Fairbanks and started teaching six shorthand students in the evening in my living room. Then the question arose, 'What good is shorthand without typing?' I accumulated ten used typewriters for my students. Then came the thought, 'What good is shorthand and typing without English and spelling?' I had no idea what I was getting into, typing taught in the kitchen and advanced dictation in a converted bedroom. Then came the divorce in 1958. Not wanting to move back to Idaho and admit defeat, I decided the school was my key to independence. Later that year, together with my daughters, I moved to Anchorage and started all over again with six shorthand students, borrowed money and a sheer determination to succeed.

Approximately a year later, after deciding to expand the school large enough to become profitable, I approached the bankers for a small business loan. The bankers took one look at me, my finances, shook their heads and told me to take bankruptcy, as no other school had ever been successful in Anchorage and I was wasting my time and money. Well, that hit me like a ton of bricks. I still felt a moral obligation to pay back all the people who had trusted me. Besides that, I didn't know how to declare bankruptcy and did not want to learn. I decided I could never disgrace myself or my family with a bankruptcy. So I hired someone smarter than myself to operate the college and earned my living by managing an employment agency and feeding the business school.

I took over an employment agency that was doing little or no business and turned it around into a very profitable employment agency, when an opportunity to buy a temporary service came along. Of course, I saw a great potential, but had no capital. I suggested that my employer buy it, and I would run it for him with the profit divided between us at an agreed upon split. It became a very profitable venture running both the permanent and the temporary side by side. One day he decided to change the percentage--more for him, less for me. He reminded me that he knew I relied on my earned income and said if I did not like it I could leave. With a slap in the face like that, after turning a nothing business into a very successful one, I decided it was time to move on. Within three months, with very little capital, I created a full time placement agency and acquired a Western Girl Temporary Help franchise.

In 1961 we moved the Alaska Business College into a better location for our students. On New Year's Day in 1964, just when the school was beginning to break even, a fire destroyed the entire building. Fire or not, I still had an obligation to the enrolled students. I contacted my publishing companies and they rushed new textbooks to us. I borrowed folding banquet tables and chairs from the Anchorage Westward Hotel. The IBM Company took trade-in typewriters ready for shipment back to the factory and loaned them to us until our new equipment arrived. I found a new location, remodeled and started over again. Less than three months later, the devastating Good Friday earthquake struck Alaska. On the morning of the earthquake, IBM had just delivered and unpacked $20,000 worth of office equipment for the business college. We were very fortunate and had only one typewriter hit the floor, but the building was seriously damaged.

During this period I had remarried. Along with my new husband came four stepchildren. After seven stormy years I gave up on this marriage. There I was, alone again, divorced again, and heavily in debt. It was probably the lowest point in my adult life -- my world was in pieces and my own self-image was at an all-time low. The bankers were recommending that I take bankruptcy, but again I had to pay back the people who had trusted me.

In 1970 we became the only nationally Accredited One Year School of Business in the State of Alaska. By 1977 the business college was in a 10,000 square foot, two-story, modern building and had an enrollment of 100 to 175 students year round. We had 12 full-time and several part-time instructors, a graduate placement department, financial aid and admissions officers. By 1983 we had phenomenal growth, successful graduates and a fantastic reputation in the community. Best of all, I was finally free of debt.

I did not know it at the time, but the man I hired as Director of the school three years earlier, who had been a friend of many years, joined together with another party to destroy our reputation so they could open their own business college. It was a crushing blow. In six months time our revenue dropped $500,000 and our reputation had been smeared. Our only survival at that time came about as a result of a Small Business Administration loan during 1984 for $315,000, which has since been paid in full. It took me six years to climb back to where we were before the vicious attack. In 1986 I moved the college into the office section of the largest shopping mall in Anchorage, the Dimond Center. Many doomsayers warned against such an outlandish place for a business college - but it felt right. It proved to be a very wise decision.

Every five years I would make a new five year plan to prepare to sell the college. Several potential buyers came and went. I would not follow up on those buyers that appeared to be in it just for the money. The college and the students were my family and if they were not going to be cared for then I would not sell. When Phillips Colleges tendered an offer to buy the institution, I knew they would fulfill my ultimate dream and become a full-fledged junior college. I sold to Phillips in 1989. On May 16, 1991 the Alaska Junior College dedicated the Alaska Junior College Bettye L. Smith Resource Learning Library in my name. I truly appreciated this great honor. Books and helping people make a better life for themselves have always been the activities where I've received the most joy.

Two weeks of retirement was enough for me. Remembering the enjoyment I had running the employment and temporary help agencies, I opened Personnel Pool of Alaska and Alaska Employment Agency. I also opened the Alaska Division of Martha Weems, Ltd., an advertising specialty sales company. I love meeting new people and learning something new every day. The advertising specialty business is the one I'll continue to operate when I decide to retire. Personnel Pool of Alaska and the Alaska Employment Agency are just beginning to take off. The future is really bright as more and more companies realize the cost effectiveness of using temporary help services and permanent employment agencies. My specialty advertising business is such fun I would like to do this 100 percent of my time.

As a result, I am considering the possibility of allowing someone else to own the Alaska Employment Agency and Personnel Pool of Alaska. As much as I love the employment service and temporary help business, I have decided it is time to slow down. I realize I can't do justice to all three businesses.

I have always enjoyed working, but my business strengths come primarily from three sources. The most important strength I have is honesty. I feel I must stick by my word even when it goes against my desires. I have paid a heavy price at times, but it has never failed to benefit me in the long run. Second in importance is knowing that the harder I work the luckier I get. Finally, I believe and rely on myself to ultimately accomplish the goals I set out to obtain.

It's just as significant to recognize one's strengths as it is to acknowledge one's weaknesses. I found problems would arise when I would believe too much in the integrity and goodness of others; however, 99 percent of the time this approach does pay off. When it doesn't I don't waste time bemoaning it but just move on to the next good person. I have learned the hard way when it comes to keeping an employee on long past the time I should have discharged him or her. My experience has proven that a person will undermine the entire company if they are allowed to stay on because you believe they will change for the better. Another weakness that used to affect me more than it does now is freely spending money -- I figured that's what it was for. I am getting a little smarter now and do not spend as freely as in the past.

As I reflect back on the business college I remind myself that without the help of others I would never have succeeded. Over the past thirty years there were three bankers without whose faith and trust I would never have survived. Above all I thank the wonderful teachers who helped establish the school's reputation. The suppliers who lent me equipment after the fire, my friends who stood by me during the down times, members of the Association of Independent Colleges and Schools that genuinely shared their success and failures with me. Their freely sharing their experiences with me has been priceless. I credit my daughters, Jerye and Marie, with keeping me young at heart and looking forward to tomorrow. I credit my mother and father with giving me a good set of values, a work ethic and faith in the future. Finally, I credit my grandmother for many things, but I remember her favorite saying that always hung by her door:

> The past is dead and gone.
> The future who can say?
> The present is ours to live and love.
> Thank God we own today!

Over the years I have seen many of the disadvantages of being a woman entrepreneur. But the past is dead and gone and I don't dwell on it. Today I believe a woman can do and be anything she wants to be and do.

Being in business for yourself is quite exciting but what surprised me most was that dedication and honesty are not always appreciated, understood or even accepted. I also noticed that becoming very successful sometimes makes you a target of small and envious individuals. I don't suppose I should have been amazed, but unfortunately, a small number of bureaucrats and a few members of the legal system are there to hinder, not help an entrepreneur.

I would recommend to a new woman entrepreneur several things. First, you need the appropriate education which includes several good accounting courses. Every difficulty you overcome is an educational experience in itself and will help you survive and make the next struggle a little easier. It is also important to work with a good accountant and to pull a financial statement each month. You will need to find and use an honest attorney for your legal counsel. Don't wait until you have a problem and then try to find a good attorney. Sometimes you will find out that it is best to take all the advice everyone has to offer, digest it, and then make your own decisions; then stand by your decisions even when 99 percent of the people are telling you what a terrible mistake you are making.

It is important to recognize that no business runs smoothly all the time. Every business has its peaks and valleys. This is a natural phenomena and it is vital to prepare yourself for the tough times. When the going gets tough, hang in there, get some expert advice and work long dedicated hours to figure out just what is needed to succeed. Focus on the fact that you will succeed if you work hard enough, long enough and believe in yourself. You must make some very hard choices if you are to succeed in business. If you cannot do that -- work for someone else. They will make your choices for you."

BETTYE L. SMITH
TEL: (907) 258-2584

JANET L. KENDRICK, M.D.

FAMILY MEDICINE

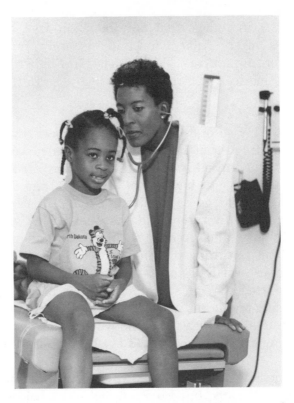

Dr. Janet Kendrick is a Family Physician in private practice in Lithonia, Georgia just east of Atlanta. At medical school an evaluating surgeon termed Janet as 'no different than any other student', but she knew she was different and has more than proved it with her dedication to her community. She once teased her father saying she was going to become a **real** doctor - and by working in churches and clinics for teens, elders and indigents, she truly has become a doctor in the purest sense of the word. Originally from New York, Dr. Kendrick received her BA degree from Oberlin College and her MD degree from the University of Cincinnati College of Medicine. Dr. Kendrick became Board Certified in Family Practice after completing her residency at Brookdale Hospital in Brooklyn, New York. She is a Diplomat of the American Academy of Family Practice and a Fellow of the American Academy of Family Physicians. While a member of the National Health Service Corps, Dr. Kendrick was awarded the State Certificate of Merit from the Governor of Arkansas for medical services provided at College Station, Arkansas.

'There was so much to worry about that I didn't know what to worry about first - so I prayed.....

I wasn't planning on becoming a physician. I was planning on taking courses in college that only met Mondays, Wednesdays and Fridays after 11:00 a.m. and certainly no 8:00 a.m. Saturday morning courses. With a major in English specializing in African American Literature one has a certain amount of leeway.

At the end of my second year I started to have serious doubts about the usefulness of my major as it related to my future ability to support myself. About that time my older sister was talking about going to law school. I said if she went to law school then I would go to medical school. There has always been a bit of healthy competition between us. I got a second major in Biology and became a 'premed' student. Organic Chemistry met Saturday morning at 8:00 a.m. I always felt that was unnecessarily ugly but I supposed it was to weed out the uncommitted. While I completed my premed courses I enjoyed teasing my father who is a psychiatrist that I was going to become a 'real' doctor. (I had no way of knowing how much psychiatry my own practice would eventually entail.)

I went to medical school at the University of Cincinnati. My presence was tolerated but I did not feel like I belonged. I will never forget the evaluation I received from an elderly white surgeon. He wrote that I was 'a calm, collected, colored girl essentially no different than any of my other students.' But I knew I **was** different.

Between undergrad and medical school, I worked as a salesgirl for a major department store in New York, a receptionist for a shipping company in San Francisco, a clerk/typist for a residential treatment center for adolescents and a teacher at a private school in Oakland. Not only was I older than most of my classmates I'd had much more living experience than they had. I think that's part of what makes the type of medicine I practice special.

134

If you come to my office for a blood pressure check you will get one, but you may find yourself telling me about the fight you had with your wife about eggs last week; or that you love your grandbaby but wish your adult-child would move out or that you can't sleep and have been drinking a little too much lately. A good deal of what my patients tell me is not what they came in to talk about, like the woman who came for a physical exam and wound up telling me that it has been hard to pray lately, or the man who's been lonely and bored since his retirement. I sit quietly, I listen, I don't judge.

Being a Family Physician means developing an ongoing relationship with the patient and hopefully the family. I treat the whole person, not just the disease. Medical problems do not occur in a vacuum; the more I know and understand about my patient's lifestyle the more I can help. Sometimes all that is involved is listening. Sometimes a referral to a service in the community is necessary. Being community-based, I am aware of what resources are available in our neighborhood whether it is an AA meeting, a local program at the YMCA, Weight Watchers, Meals on Wheels or the Senior Citizen Center.

One of the questions I'm often asked is how a New Yorker wound up practicing medicine in Georgia. Like many of my colleagues I didn't have enough money to finance my medical education. My mother helped me with tuition and I also borrowed money from the government through the National Health Service Corps scholarship program. At the beginning of medical school in the summer of 1978 it seemed like a wonderful idea. The government would pay for my tuition, books and living expenses for two years. In return I agreed to pay them back by practicing in a Health Manpower Shortage Area for two years.

In Brooklyn, the summer of 1982 when payback time came around it seemed less like a wonderful idea and more like indentured servitude. I was married to a man who was in law school in New York and I was eight months pregnant. I tried without success to get a deferment or be allowed to serve my time in a HMSA in New York. I wanted to have my baby in New York and be with my husband. My baby was due on July

31st. I was supposed to start fulfilling my NHSC obligation in Arkansas on July 1st. I was allowed to remain in New York until my daughter was born. Two weeks later I was in Arkansas preparing to be the Medical Director of College Station Clinic. College Station is a small, poor, rural town about 20 minutes outside of Little Rock.

Despite the difficulties of being on call every night and caring for a newborn infant, I managed to survive. One of my major accomplishments was to get a new cesspool for the clinic. This was vital because when it rained the toilets would overflow and could not be used. Spearheaded by my outrage that any medical facility could possibly be operating under such unsanitary conditions in this country, several of the local churches got together and raised enough money to replace the old cesspool.

Largely because of my positive experience with the Corps and several black physician role models in the community, I developed enough self-confidence to consider setting up my own practice. After I had been back in New York for two years I decided it was time. New York was getting to be too much for me and I wanted to move back down South. To those of us in the North, Atlanta was the mecca where all dreams could come true.

After a few false starts I eventually had not only a dream but a medical consultant, a business plan and potential office space in Lithonia, Georgia. Finally, after being turned down by several banks, one young female banker agreed to loan me $70,000. That was $30,000 short of what my business plan called for but it was a start. I figured I could finesse the rest. On the strength of a verbal commitment from the banker I moved to Georgia.

At this point I was legally separated, had custody of my four-year-old-daughter and a few thousand dollars in savings. A month after I moved to Georgia, the bank reneged on my loan. It was October 1989 and there I was stranded in Georgia with no family except a four-year-old child. I had no daycare, no job, no Georgia medical license (applied for but still pending) and

136

my savings were rapidly being depleted. There was so much to worry about that I didn't know what to worry about first; there was every reason to pray. Life was very difficult but I prayed constantly; in the car, on the way to meetings, at home, in church. I thanked Him for all His blessings and I asked Him to take care of us. My philosophy of life was simple -- Pray More, Worry Less. (It is impossible to do both at the same time.) By December I had daycare, my Georgia medical license, three jobs and a loan from the Small Business Administration to open my practice.

Holding three jobs meant I used to take my daughter to daycare in the morning, go to my day job, pick her up at 6:00 p.m. to take her to nightcare and go to my Emergency Room job. On the weekends I had a thirteen-year-old neighbor come watch her so I could go to my third job.

The best business decision I ever made was to go into private practice. The worst was to be totally unprepared for the length of time it would take the business to become viable and not to have saved enough capital prior to starting. It was distressing to spend so much time away from my daughter and I would never choose to do that again. Like most working mothers I constantly felt the pressure of needing to be in at least three places at once. Thankfully things are much easier now. I had a wonderful family and friends who were very supportive and they filled in for me whenever necessary. Because of their support I was able to turn my dream into a reality."

Editor's Note: Dr. Kendrick was recommended to us by the SBA office in Atlanta, Georgia because of her dedication to helping her community. She did not "toot her own horn" but the SBA did. According to them her success is not measured in dollars, but in good works.

JANET L. KENDRICK, M.D.
3598 Panola Road, Lithonia, GA 30038
TEL: (404) 593-9413

JUDEE SLACK, EA, CFP
SLACK & ASSOCIATES

Judee Slack, Slack & Associates, is an Enrolled Agent and Certified Financial Planner. What began as a simple bookkeeping service quickly expanded to include tax preparation, financial planning and investment counseling. The firm occupies the entire 2nd story of Judee's home and is the living proof that a home-based business can look professional, be professional, and exude credibility. The firm has succeeded because of Judee's strong commitment to understanding and serving the needs of her customers. She is currently in the forefront of a growing coalition that has been formed to benefit businesses that use independent contractors. Judee believes in education as an ongoing process and her current goal is a Master of Science in Taxation. She is involved in several community organizations and is the Vice President of Finance for the Orange County Chapter of NAWBO. More importantly -- Judee is the only accountant we know who never works on April 15th. Instead this unique lady celebrates by throwing a catered champagne party for her clients.

"Listen to what your clients are saying and, perhaps what they're not saying.....

People think of accountants as uncaring 'bean counters' who keep their noses buried in a set of books. The challenge of overcoming this stereotype led me to add creativity to what I do. By expanding my business to fit my clients' growing needs and by putting some fun into it, I have established myself as someone who cares about more than just numbers.

On April 15, when most tax preparers cram their last forms into envelopes to be rushed to the IRS, I celebrate the end of the grueling tax season by throwing a catered, champagne party for my clients. We staged the 'first annual' party in 1987 and it is now a tradition. One of my long-time clients hasn't missed a party yet, and his wife told me at the last one that he looks forward to it all year. The party also serves as an excellent excuse to say no to what was becoming a growing number of procrastinators, knocking on my door April 15th with that desperate look in their eyes. I used to say yes, when doing 'just one more' tax return was the last thing I wanted to do. But you can't do a tax return when you're planning a party, right? My party received special attention this year when the Orange County Register ran a story on the front page of the business section. So you see, accountants do have personalities!

I started my business after 8 years of balancing full time work at a CPA firm, the demanding duties of being a wife, and the responsibility of being a mother to a young son. I knew my son was becoming a 'latchkey kid', and this bothered me. Also, when you work for someone else, you do all the work and they get all the money! This is when I decided to start my own accounting practice.

From the very beginning I decided that if I wanted to become a successful businesswoman I was going to have to be better than the men who were my contemporaries. My first step was to take the comprehensive Enrolled Agent exam, given only once a year by the IRS. Since only about 30% of those taking the exam pass it, I felt extremely proud to be in that elite group.

I was qualified as a tax expert and could represent taxpayers before the IRS, a factor that would greatly enhance my business.

Even though my office is home-based, I pride myself on its professional look. Most home offices consist of a dining room table cluttered with paperwork and a computer. My husband and I live in a five bedroom home, three bedrooms upstairs and two downstairs. The entire upstairs is office space. I use the largest room as my office; it is lined with oak bookcases and cabinetry to hold the many reference books that tax people love(?) so much. Literature describing various investments or pertinent tax information sits on a table for clients' use. The rest of the rooms are used to house my staff. Each desk is equipped with an up-to-date computer and other office equipment. This image is imperative to anyone wanting to attract and keep good clients.

Although working at home allowed me to be there when my son returned from school, I learned at the outset that when you work out of your home no one really thinks you work. Even my husband frequently asked me, 'When are you going to get a real job?' Also, friends and relatives called regularly during my work hours to chit chat because they pictured me sitting at home doing nothing. I'm happy to say that after 10 years of watching me enjoy the freedom and self-fulfillment of calling my own shots, my husband quit his 'real' job and now works with me. Even my friends and relatives have watched my business flourish and now know better than to call during working hours just to pass the time of day.

I started my practice in 1979, and as my clients' needs expanded, so did my services. During the 1980's, people bombarded by the buzzwords of the day, tax shelters and tax-saving investments, came to me with many questions. Most people do not know that the typical accounting educational requirements do not cover investment products.

In order to help my clients, and to establish myself as more than just a tax preparer, I enrolled in the Certified Financial Planner Program. This program covers all types of investments, insurance, retirement, estate planning, as well as tax planning. To be able to implement a client's financial plan, I qualified for a Securities Series Seven license (allowing me to sell stocks and mutual funds), a real estate license, and a life and disability insurance license. Now we can unbiasedly advise clients in all areas and execute the appropriate investment.

The issue of independent contractors is fast becoming the hot topic of the 1990's. When you hire an employee, you have to pay payroll taxes, which can be a huge burden on the small business person. Using an independent contractor allows you to avoid this. There is nothing wrong with hiring and classifying them as such, as long as they fit the IRS's definition. Unfortunately, a few companies mask employees as independent contractors and try to sneak them by the IRS.

The IRS, of course, got wise to this. But in their quest to find those doing wrong, their giant shovel is scooping up what seems to be every small business person and landing them with an audit. It's like using a sledgehammer to smash one ant and killing all of them in a ten mile radius. Of those being audited, 92% are being forced to pay back taxes, penalties and interest, with the average amount owed being $30,000. What a gold mine for the IRS!

To help several clients caught under this black umbrella, I got involved. We are forming a non-profit organization for small businesses opposed to restrictive regulations regarding the use of independent contractors. With the assistance of several legislators and a lobbyist in Sacramento, we succeeded in postponing proposed EDD regulations that are detrimental to a specific industry. The goal of our growing coalition is to benefit all businesses that use independent contractors.

Because the laws affecting my business are constantly changing, continual education has always been a priority. Getting professional designations and licenses helped promote my practice, but it also cut into time allowed for formal education. Although it took me 25 years, I finally completed my Bachelor of Science in Business Administration in May of 1991. My current education goal is a Master of Science in Taxation.

Clients frequently need help throughout the year regarding the tax consequences of both day-to-day transactions and major decisions such as buying or selling their homes or businesses. In addition to having solid knowledge, a good tax advisor needs strong personal rapport with her clients. When you deal with people's money, you not only get into their finances, you get into all areas of their life - professional problems, personal problems, problems with their kids, everything. A woman has the advantage over a man in this area. Women are natural care givers, especially those who have weathered the experience of raising children.

My recommendation to women entrepreneurs is to always live by the golden rule, 'Do unto others as you would have them do unto you'. By treating your clients with care and respect you will receive more referrals and returns than you can handle. You must also listen to what your clients are saying, and perhaps what they're not saying. Most people are much too busy talking to listen to others. As Booker T. Washington once said, **'Excellence is to do a common thing in an uncommon way.'"**

SLACK & ASSOCIATES
8941 Gleneagles Circle, Westminster, CA 92683
TEL: (714) 891-0731

LYNDA MILLIGAN & NANCY SMITH

GREAT AMERICAN QUILT FACTORY, INC.

"The Great American Quilt Factory, Inc." in Denver, Colorado was founded in 1981 by Lynda Milligan, President (standing), and Nancy Smith, Secretary-Treasurer (seated). The two met at a quilting symposium in 1977. They began their company with a borrowed initial investment of $35,000 and now have annual sales of over $1.5 million. They have 20 employees and export their products to Europe and Canada. Making quilts was not enough. Lynda and Nancy also diversified with "DreamSpinners", making and selling over 250,000 patterns a year for baby quilts, soft dolls, teddy bears, and home decorating items. The third arm of their company is a publishing company. They named it "Possibilities" -- symbolic of the freedom they have to choose new directions for their business.

"When Lynda and I attended a quilting symposium in Oregon 14 years ago, little did we know how our lives would become intertwined.....

It was the first trip either of us had taken on our own and we both did a lot of soul searching and dream sharing. One of Lynda's dreams was to open her own quilt and fabric store. The mention of that dream was a seed that was planted in the minds of two women, both ready and needing to grow. On an evening walk, after one of the lectures, we wandered into a convenience store in Ashland. We laugh at how we both emerged at the counter with the same two items - a bottle of wine and a Dreamsicle. That was the beginning of our discovering how well our minds mesh.

When we returned to Denver we found ourselves in very different situations. Lynda's marriage was shaky and I was feeling a need to stretch the boundaries of wife and mother. We would meet every so often and our talks would always seem to come back to the subject of a quilt shop. We started to plan, dreaming of how wonderful and desirable 'our' little shop would be.

I don't recall when our daydreams turned into goals, but we developed a business plan, selected a site and filled out purchase orders for inventory. When we were ready we approached Lynda's father-in-law, a self-made man, owner of his own business, and a proponent of entrepreneurs. He agreed to lend us our start-up investment and we were on our way. We negotiated (ha ha) and signed our first lease. The daydream was over!

Neither of us had a business background. I was educated to be a social worker at the University of Michigan in my home state, and Lynda had graduated from the University of Northern Colorado (Greeley), planning to become an elementary school teacher.

We didn't let that stop us, in fact, we lacked enough business intelligence to know that the odds were against our success.

146

We treated our investment as a business from day one. We have always paid ourselves a salary - even though there were many weeks that the paychecks couldn't be cashed. We garnered help and advice from the people closest to us.

One of our first employees, Ruth Haggbloom, who lives in the southeast Denver neighborhood of our shop, sauntered in on one of her afternoon walks. She was taking a quilting class through Denver Opportunity School and was interested in what we carried. After talking with us and discovering that neither of us lived very close to the store, she volunteered to open up for us if the weather delayed us. We thought that it was a marvelous idea, although we didn't know where she would get the key. A week later we hired her for a part time sales position which she holds to this day. Another woman, Sharon Holmes, was hired because we knew her well enough to ask (desperately) if she would help cut fabric during our first sale. She calmly tucked her three year old boy under the cutting table with a book and proceeded to help us. She now helps us edit and proofread patterns and books. Much of our success is due to the loyalty, creativity and pride of our employees.

After about three years in business we met Dick Rogers, an accountant that specialized in small businesses. We interviewed him and decided very quickly that he was someone we wanted on our team. Dick has seen us through thick and thin - and believe me, times got pretty tight in Denver in the mid-80's when Colorado's recession was behind only Texas for strength and scope. Dick has been one of the primary reasons for our successful expansion and diversifications. He helped us to see that we needed to let go of having our hands in everything and to delegate. One of the ways he helped us was by asking us to think of what else we could be doing to generate income if we let someone else take over a specific job or department. He helped us to realize that other people could do the job, maybe not exactly like we would do it, but probably with the same results. This allowed us to invest our time more wisely.

Our first step on the road to diversification was designing baby quilt patterns. Our customers were requesting patterns that were unavailable in the market at that time. DreamSpinner patterns were designed to fill this niche. From baby quilts to soft dolls, teddy bears, and home decorating items, the DreamSpinner line grew to become the most recognized pattern line in the industry, selling well over 250,000 patterns a year. Lynda and I both love to design and create new products. Since 1985 we have added at least eight original patterns a year to the line.

Our newest endeavor is in publishing. Lynda and I are constantly brain storming about other facets of the quilting business that we haven't tried as well as a myriad of other business adventures that we would like to try. We needed a new name for this arm of our company and while we were wandering the streets of York, PA we thought of it... POSSIBILITIES ... what better name to give us the freedom to choose a new direction for our business.

As our business has grown our staffing needs have also grown. We employ twenty people and have hired our first mid-level manager this year, a vice president of marketing and management. We are finding a need to departmentalize our staff. We're encouraging our employees to grow with the company by investing in their continued education, be it computer, customer service, art, or quilting classes. We offer retirement benefits and a profit-sharing plan. These plans were suggested by our accountant, Dick Rogers, at the appropriate time.

Between us we manage households with five children. Lynda's husband works for Storage Tek and mine is a district judge. Our business has grown up with our families; along the way we've tried to embrace the needs of our families and our employees. Playpens and cribs were part of the decor in the early days. Hours have been flexible to allow for sick children as well as school programs and summer vacations.

What we've done is commit to our own growth. We're always studying our industry and taking classes that stretch us to achieve our potential. Self help books. audio tapes, and seminars have become an important part of our lives. We go through model-making exercises with Dick Rogers to envision certain scenarios. That helps us make the critical choices with greater consciousness of potential outcomes. Perhaps our most important strength is in our energy as a team. We feed off of each other's energy. Together, we believe we're greater than the sum of our parts. After all these years we still 'click' together - as long as we're communicating. If we get too sidetracked and forget our goals, we lose ground. And if we lose track of our 'selves', getting back to basics - actually sewing a quilt, for instance, not just supervising the sewing of one - gets us back in sync.

While Lynda is motivated by dollars and cents (she regularly figures out what salary she would like to be making and works backward from there to see what sales have to be), I am motivated by recognition for achievement. We both have a need for respect, respect for a job well done. With the terrific team that supports us, how can we lose!"

THE GREAT AMERICAN QUILT FACTORY, INC.
DREAMSPINNERS, POSSIBILITIES
8970 E. Hampden, Denver, Colorado 80231
TEL: (303) 740-6206, FAX: (303) 220-7424

KATHY BRESSLER

CATTLE KATE

Kathy Bressler, alias "Cattle Kate", makes clothing in the style of the Old West in Wilson, Wyoming near Jackson Hole. She is 41 and lives in a small log cabin with her husband of 13 years and her daughter who is ten. She has a horse, dog and cat. Kathy spends her free time in the mountains and on the surrounding lakes and rivers with her family. She attended Colorado State University in Fort Collins, Colorado for one year. In 1972 she graduated from the National Outdoor Leadership School in the Wind River Mountain Range. For the next 8 years Kathy lived in a tiny semi-ghost town of 45 people. She sewed clothes, surveyed roads, worked on an oil rig, taught dancing and baked bread for a living. In 1981 she borrowed $300 from her husband and made silk scarves. She added dresses and accessories to her line and marketed through trade shows and catalogs. Kathy's story is one of uncontrolled growth coupled with a lack of management skills. Although her products were selling well, she nearly lost everything. Not one to be defeated, she reorganized and, with effective management, has turned her business around. Today she has a 24-page catalog, 40-60 products, 4 full-time employees, 8 home-based seamstresses and contractors for large runs of her most popular products.

"And so my years in South Pass were the beginning of my love of the old West.....

I first acquired the name 'Cattle Kate' from my friends in the South Pass area of Wyoming. I was one of two single girls that lived there at the time and the other girl's nickname was Calamity Jane. Atlantic City was a tiny semi-ghost town of 45 people with the Red Desert to the south, the Windriver Mountains to the north and the Old Oregon Trail just a few miles from town. The area was full of history and had at one time been a booming gold mining town. Many old buildings and remnants of the past still remained. I lived there for about eight years, winter and summer, and loved every minute of it.

Atlantic City, (named so because it is on the Atlantic side of the Continental Divide), became for me a step back in time. My closest friends and I lived the old way, no running water, no electricity, gathered our own wood in the fall to keep us warm through the winter and sometimes shot our own deer, elk or antelope to feed us. The Mercantile Saloon was one of few public businesses in town and became the local meeting place and dance hall. I loved to dance and had always made my own clothes.

So, to go along with the old west feeling there, I started making full skirts and petticoats, etc., to go dancing in. Pretty soon I was making clothes for my girl friends to dance in and then opened a small shop in the corner of the establishment to sew for money. In the winter I made down coats and vests and in the summer, old style full skirted dance clothes. The shop was fun but with only 45 people to sew for, it didn't last long.

When living in such a limited job area, you need to do whatever comes along to make a living. Even though it didn't cost much to live that lifestyle, I still had to work and was able to acquire some interesting experiences. To name a few: I was a surveyor on the Red Desert; I was the first woman to work at the Atlantic City Iron Ore mine; I baked bread for the town; I taught folk dancing on a small scale; I ran the general store one summer at South Pass City; I was a roughneck on an oil rig, and occasionally I had to move away for a couple of months in the winter to make enough money to carry me through to the summer. The six mile dirt road sometimes closed from the South Pass highway into Atlantic City in the winter because of heavy snow storms. This made it necessary to either stay at home in our cabins or ski back and forth to the highway, assuming you had a car waiting.

The one thing I loved the most about my time back in time, was the people. There were all ages and all types, but we were all there by choice and that choice of lifestyle bound us together in a special way. I have never been around a group of people that had more fun; worked harder when they wanted to; or looked out for each other more. Looking back, I am very impressed and privileged. And so my years in South Pass were the beginning of my love of the old west and many years later 'Cattle Kate' became a way for me to keep that love alive and to share that lifestyle with others.

I met and married David Bressler in 1978. David was a fishing guide on the Snake River at that time. He now owns and operates Bressler Insulation and the Double Diamond Glove Company. I had my daughter, Jenny, in 1981 and after my pregnancy, I was anxious to get life back to normal. A friend of mine suggested making western scarves because she owned a retail store and knew there was a demand for them that was not being met.

I decided to start a small business. I borrowed $300.00 from my husband, did some research and bought a minimum amount of silk in 3 or 4 different colors. At first I sold to friends and friends of friends. David and his hunting buddies especially liked the warmth of the silk around the neck. Soon they were selling at a rapid pace.

I decided to go wholesale to the local stores in Jackson Hole. That went over well and someone suggested I take out an ad in the back of Western Horseman Magazine which I did. The first ad was done by me with a picture of my husband in a 'Cattle Kate' scarf. The picture was so blurred and unprofessional it caught people's eye. We were really in business now. I was selling retail through the mail and western stores across the country were calling to see if I would wholesale to them.

The first one and a half to two years I was a one woman operation. I bought 50 yard bolts of silk, tore it to size, and used my Juki industrial sewing machine my father-in-law gave us as a wedding present to sew them up. All of this was done in my small living room with my baby daughter playing with the silk scraps in the corner. Soon I hired part-time home workers to help out.

The scarves were easy. They came in beautiful colors of silk, they were one size, simple to make, and easy to sell. I was having fun and making good money. Things just kept growing and the natural progression for me was to expand into making dance clothing. I was having so much fun creating that it just seemed to be the next step in my business. A friend and employee took my scarves to a wholesale western apparel show in Dallas, TX and I thought I'd throw in a couple of dresses to see what kind of response I'd get. The response was good enough but the feedback was that I needed a full line, not just two dresses. So I came up with a small line of clothing and accessories and put them into a small black and white catalogue. I started going to trade shows and sending the catalogue out all over the country.

I was driven by the excitement and the freedom to create. Never had I had so much fun sharing the creative parts of my personality. In the beginning all I did was create. The business I was growing was still in its early stages. However, I was not aware of exactly what I was creating. Little did I realize that pretty soon I would be responsible for a fast growing 'big' (compared to anything I'd done before) business, with all the employees needed to run it, and management skills needed to make it work.

The business grew by leaps and bounds and pretty soon it was more than I knew how to deal with and I needed help I couldn't afford. I was running into cash flow problems because of uncontrolled growth. I was and still am better at creating and being creative than managing a business. I had to learn the hard way. I have learned much and still have a long way to go.

Last year I hired a business consultant who seemed to be doing good things for the business. I was overwhelmed and just wanted someone to take the management away so that I could just do more designing. I made the mistake of turning over all management to this consultant and pretty much going along with whatever he wanted to do. He had BIG plans but what we really needed was to slow things down. He spent lots of money I did not have and cut prices on all my products. That was the year I lost $100,000. We got through it, but had to completely reorganize. We laid off six out of nine people, discontinued our representative program and rented out one-half of our building.

David and I had personally guaranteed all the 'Cattle Kate' loans and we were afraid of losing everything. But with the help of a few key people we recovered and at the present time have stabilized and are making a profit.

A couple of months ago I hired another consultant who was able to lead me in the right direction this time. With his help I feel I can balance the areas in which I'm weak and learn how to manage effectively. We have never had a problem selling our product. Our challenge has always been managing a small, somewhat complicated, fast growing manufacturing business.

Presently, we are planning our next catalogue run which will be our 4th catalogue. We now have a 24 page catalogue and sell approximately 40-60 products. Most of the products offered in our catalogue are made and designed by me and my staff.

I enjoy researching clothing, customs, and styles of the old west. The detail in construction of old clothing is amazing in itself. Our clothing is mostly sewn by home seamstresses and then sent back to us for quality control and finishing touches. At the present time we have four full-time employees at headquarters and between 6-8 seamstresses sewing at home. Some of our more popular products are sewn by contractors in runs of 100-500 pieces.

We are very proud of the reputation we have for design and quality. I believe one of our biggest challenges is to keep our high standard of quality as we grow. However, we seem to be doing it.

My business has been an incredible challenge in my life. It has caused me to be physically and mentally ill and it has also allowed me total freedom in ways I never expected. I am proud of the accomplishment. I love being able to share what I love with others."

CATTLE KATE'S
P.O. Box 572, Wilson, WY 83014
TEL: (307) 733-7414, FAX: (307) 739-0767

DR. JEANNE MORRIS MURRAY
SEQUOIA ASSOCIATES, INC.

Dr. Jeanne Morris Murray became an entrepreneur later in life, forming with her husband and two long time friends a think tank called Sequoia Associates. Even as a young girl, Jeanne faced and overcame obstacles - many that no longer exist - of being a woman in the business and intellectual world. She decided early on to break down walls of traditional thinking quietly and unobtrusively, choosing to direct her energies towards her own advancement. Jeanne holds three degrees: B.S. in mathematics from Morris Harvey College (1957); M.S. in Information and Computer Science from Georgia Institute of Technology (1966); Ph.D. in Public Administration and Technology of Management, The American University (1981). Her commitment to educating herself in a wide variety of disciplines keeps Sequoia Associates on the cutting edge of solving both today's and tomorrow's complex problems.

Life has always been fascinating and exciting. My sister and I grew up under the benefits of our parents' devotion to the Montessori Method of bringing up children. Early in life we were taught that one of the most wonderful things to do was to learn, and we were exposed to learning at a young age. We read at two years, we were opera and ballet goers at three years, and there was always music in our home. Both of our parents danced, sang, and played music with their friends and relatives, including us. I learned to use my father's drawing table and instruments at five, made myself a dress at six, and we swam, went camping, hiked, did tumbling exercises and ballet, shot arrows with small bows, were taught to use firearms and learned to make fabulous candy. There never was any 'store candy' in our home, we made our own.

The joy of participating as a team member in my father's small business began when I was eight years old (what would the child labor folks think of that!) He offered me 'folding money' to make templates for the large letters in WESTERN ELECTRIC for the sign that was to be cast in concrete and placed across the front of a new building he was constructing. He later drove me past the finished building and there was the sign with my letters on it. And I could say, 'Look what we did!'

I married quite young. After I had three children I decided to pursue a degree in mathematics. Because of the demands of a family I couldn't begin my studying until after 11:00 at night. If I had a quiz the next day I didn't go to bed. Consequently, I learned to get by on very little sleep.

After graduation from college, I worked for the next nine years on the research faculty at Georgia Tech. I was the second female research scientist in the history of the university and they didn't die from it! My advice to the few female freshmen students was, 'Look like a woman, think like a man, work like a dog, and act like a lady.' This was not original. I had read it somewhere, but I thought it made sense and lived by it. Throughout my career there were difficulties because I was a woman in a man's field. I just accepted this as a reality and didn't waste energy banging my head against a wall. I always considered it a privilege to work with those people.

During my career I have worked for industry, universities, and the government. When I finished my PhD in 1981, I remembered the fun and satisfaction of working in my father's small business and decided to form one of my own. My husband and two friends of long standing worked with me to set up the firm. The four of us are now stockholders and principals of the corporation.

Three of the principals in our firm have Cherokee ancestors, so we decided to use the word, 'Sequoia' in our business title. Sequoia was a Cherokee Indian. He invented the encoding of the Cherokee language as a phonetic syllabary. This gave the American Indians a written language. The Indians considered Sequoia the wisest of their people and they honored him by associating him with the giant California redwood tree called the Sequoia. As a tribute to this enterprising man of science, we named our firm Sequoia Associates, Inc.

Because of commitments to a large family, to my own personal interests and growth, and to the development and growth of Sequoia, we made the decision to headquarter our corporation in our home. We are lucky to live in a large dwelling in Arlington, Virginia, that overlooks a wooded nature area. There is a fifty-foot waterfall in the ravine below the house and we have deer in the back yard. Surprisingly we are only a ten minute drive from downtown Washington, D.C.

To keep at the cutting edge in several rapidly changing fields, as well as for my own personal interests, it is imperative to use time effectively. By combining my primary activities in one location, I can avoid commuting time, take care of my business interests, fulfill my role as a central figure in a large family and pursue my personal studies and interests without spending time running around from place to place.

Just off the dining room we have enclosed a screen porch with Anderson windows and put down carpeting, etc., to provide an office with an entrance directly from the carport. When one of our prospective clients asked us if we could accommodate a wheelchair, I told him 'Yes' and had a ramp installed before he arrived. The dining room, with its large table, serves as a conference room. There are other offices located in convenient parts of the house. We also have personnel cleared for TOP SECRET and codeword access. Our building has electronic security measures and we have automatic telephone intervention in case security is violated.

Sequoia Associates is best described as a think tank, and we do a lot of scientific research and studies. Sequoia's interests are broad, covering a variety of areas, including Information and Computer Sciences, Human Development and Behavior, Economics, Biomedical Research, Public Administration, Strategic Planning and Corporate Security System Design, to name a few.

George Washington University's Small Business Legal Clinic designed the firm's structure to enable us to bring in selected teams of experts. These are often drawn from the Washington Metropolitan's vast reservoir of outstanding experts and executives as associates (legally, independent contractors), to work on specific projects. In addition, each of Sequoia's four principals are educated and experienced in many disciplines and each is proficient in several of our functional areas.

We are ready to provide appropriate groups of specialists to assist in solving today's complex problems, and to work with clients to design new methods for solving tomorrow's problems. A lot of our work is government contracting. For example, we did a two and one-half year personality assessment project with the Federal Emergency Management Agency in which we studied and analyzed how people behave under increasing stress. Will they follow government policy for taking care of emergencies, or will they go to pieces? Personnel who worked on the project included about eighteen professionals, psychologists, economists, statisticians, computer experts and management scientists. In addition there were numbers of graduate students who worked on a six month literature search and other tasks required by the sponsor. The Final Report on the project was widely distributed and copies went to the NATO countries.

Another area we work in is very advanced technology and how it is transferred to other countries. For example, can a technology used in peacetime be applied militarily? There are about 400 technologies, 20 of which are considered critical. We trace them, researching new discoveries about computers and computer components, and very advanced programming. In a nutshell, we handle the marketing of high technology in the presence of defense technology controls.

Sequoia is also frequently called into the private sector to work on policy level problems. Prospective clients know they need long range planning but don't know how to effectively go about it. We come in and do a problem scenario, then design the idea scenario to help companies get to where they would like to be. Our approach begins with top management. However, we also design and teach special courses that extend the length of the administrative ladder.

Sequoia is unique in that we do not advertise or promote our business in the typical ways. We are not listed in the phone book. We get most of our business through referrals and through our associations with many professional organizations. (Ex: The Personality Assessment System Foundation, The Institute for Electrical and Electronics Engineers).

Until recently, Sequoia did not handle a lot of contracts at one time. Now, however, business is growing rapidly and we have people approaching us to tackle a number of projects. In fact, we just finished writing three proposals for very advanced software packages for research on the space program.

My philosophy of life is this: I hold the viewpoint that there are order and purpose in the universe. I believe it follows that there exists a Devine Designer and Builder who created the universe; that the purpose of Humankind is to counter the forces of entropy by living in a way that brings about order, structure, harmony and beauty in human relationships and in the environment that sustains us all...physically and spiritually and intellectually.

Although my work may appear to be very 'high tech', I want women to know that anything is possible, if they are willing to work hard and channel their energies in the right way."

Editors note: In 1988 Dr. Murray was an invited scientist to the People's Republic of China where she gave presentations on the application of strategic planning and system sciences to solving their problems. In October of 1991 (as we go to press) she will join a large group of scientists from twenty countries on a journey to Russia where they will meet with officials and scientists in Moscow and other cities. Their purpose will be to help improve the human condition through use of a whole collection of scientific applications.

SEQUOIA ASSOCIATES, INC.
P.O. Box 204
Arlington, Virginia 22210

BEVERLY DURAN

CARRETAS, THE CART COMPANY

Beverly Duran is President of Carretas, The Cart Company and The Retail Group Ltd. Ms. Duran received her BA from Harvard University in 1982 and attended Boston College Law School. While at Harvard she formulated her ideas for her company while working for a pushcart vendor in Boston's Faneuil Hall. She started three and a half years ago, with $1200 and in her parents' backyard. The company now employs thirty cartwrights and has sales of 1.7 million. Ms. Duran is dedicated to helping Hispanic youth and single mothers attain their dreams. She was the 1989 Maxie Anderson Small Business Award recipient of the Greater Albuquerque Chamber of Commerce, was named New Mexico Small Business Person for 1990, received the Outstanding Entrepreneur Award for 1990 from the National Association of Investment Companies and was presented the Distinguished Award of Excellence from the National Minority Advisory Committee of the U.S. Small Business Administration. She is the mother of two, Steven Lucero, Vice-President of Marketing at Carretas and Tamara, a pre-med student at the University of New Mexico.

"The difference between dreams and fantasies is that dreams are attainable and fantasies are not.....

There are only three ingredients you need: a true passion, an undying belief in yourself, and raw and unbridled perseverance. It's really quite simple.

In 1979, as a single mother of two small children with no money, I applied and was accepted to Harvard University as an undergraduate. In spite of all the nay sayers, I believed I could do it. It was not easy but nothing in life really is. Armed with a scholarship and money for a roof over our heads, I only had to worry about food on the table and finding sufficient hours in the day to study. The equation for success became quite simple and manageable, and I did it.

When I was a young child, my father told me that I should approach every job with enthusiasm and to do more than what I was paid for. He told me that if one made $1.00 an hour in wages, to put in $5.00 or $10.00 an hour worth of work and to always work more hours than expected, because the wise person will learn more and this will serve them well in other endeavors. Basically he was telling me to give more than I received and to keep my eyes open. This advice has served me well. I have always found an opportunity in every employment situation and I remembered my father's words when I moved back East.

Because of my responsibilities I could only work odd jobs such as catering and cashiering. I worked briefly for a cart vendor in Boston's Faneuil Hall and this opportunity led me to do what I do today, manufacture pushcarts, kiosks, and fixtures. That pushcart, the humblest means of trade, soon had me dreaming of selling chili and chili-theme products from a cart well before the chili craze had hit the United States. I also began to see that this new industry of 'Specialty Retailing' on carts and kiosks would expand and grow and that all mall developers would embrace this idea as a way to make additional revenue without large capital expenditures by utilizing the centers' common area.

164

Being poor has its advantages. I could not afford to travel to New Mexico by airlines. We had to drive. My children and I would take a different route each time and we would stop at malls along the way. One thing became clear. If major mall developers did embrace this concept of temporary tenancy in their centers, the units, carts and kiosks would have to be made to fit with the architecture of the mall. Hence, another idea of starting a manufacturing company to provide those 'architecturally correct' units. Did I have a life-long desire to start this type of business? No. It was an outgrowth of my experience.

But I never lost sight of the idea to sell chili and chili products from pushcarts and realized that my love, my true passion, was retailing. I tried to get financial backing in New Mexico for this idea but failed. I could see the heads nod with disbelief. So I completed my degree and enrolled in Boston College Law School. In the meantime my children were accepted to Milton Academy and Dana Hall, two prep schools on the East Coast and they also began the pursuit of their dreams. Graduate school is much different than undergraduate and though I received a scholarship, it was not sufficient to pay the rent. I could not financially afford a law degree and help my children. Returning to New Mexico, that pesky little pushcart idea once again resurfaced and I went for it.

My son postponed his college career and together we formed Carretas, The Cart Company. We moved in with my parents and began making pushcarts in our backyard. At night we would read everything that might aid us in our marketing efforts. We researched pushcart program development, visual display, product development, architectural design and information on the mall industry. We sat in a mall in El Paso, Texas on and off for six months studying the shopping habits of people who shopped from carts, the quality and dimensions of the units, and the products purchased from carts. We used this information to formulate our own designs, units that were functional for the vendor, attractive for the mall and affordable to the developer. Today, Carretas is four and a half years young, occupies a 26,000 square foot facility, employs thirty cartwrights and has sales of 1.7 million.

We have learned a great deal in four and a half years but more importantly, we know how much more we need to learn. We are dedicated to the mall industry and believe that carts, kiosks and temporary in-line spaces will expand and develop in the years to come. We are designing new concepts for temporary in-line spaces that we believe will change the industry.

I have not changed the way that I perceive opportunities, keeping my eyes and mind open to new developments. My dream is retailing and I believe that I have the concepts for a national chain and once again need the financing. We will get it. And when we are successful, my goal is to help Hispanic youth and women entrepreneurs attain their dreams."

CARRETAS, The Cart Company
1900 Seventh St. N.W., Albuquerque, NM 87102
TEL: (505) 764-0047, 1-800-999-1569, FAX: (505) 764-9245

LINDA WIESTER

CLEANY BOPPERS, INC.

Linda Wiester is the founder and president of CLEANY BOPPERS, INC. in Randallstown, Md., a complete commercial and residential cleaning service with carpet and floor care, **and her company does windows.** She is the mother of two children, Deby and Tommy, and grandmother of one, Amber Rose. She is currently president of the National Association of Women Business Owners, Baltimore Chapter, member of Building Service Contractors Association, Liberty Road Development Center, and Chamber of Commerce. Linda has been working with the U.S. Small Business Administration and Maryland Small Business Development Center Network for the past year counseling Women Business Owners in rural areas. Linda and her company have been featured in area newspapers and in the November 1990 and June 1991 issues of Entrepreneurial Woman and the April 1991 issue of Family Circle Magazine.

"What I didn't know is you get the test first -- and the lesson later.....

Double jeopardy! Imagine, working for your boss by day in her business and by night in her home. Not only was I a waitress in a local restaurant, but I also agreed to clean my employer's home on my day off as a personal favor to her. Now I was being evaluated in a whole new area. So, with some fears and a great deal of care, I entered a new world. I was making judgments about the household needs of another and applying my own organizational and cleaning skills to her needs. That day opened up a new direction in my life.

For years I, like so many other women in America, worked for others. Today, I am the owner of a small business, part of the growing phenomenon in Maryland. I have joined the ranks of the risk takers.

My business, CLEANY BOPPERS, INC., is a direct outgrowth of my first housecleaning job in 1978. That first job was done as a favor to a friend. Little by little my reputation required me to enlist the help of my daughter to keep up with new requests. I did not wake up one day and decide to start a business; the business just evolved. As it grew, we learned more about business.

Since the number of two-career couples was growing, I was faced with an ever-increasing demand for our services. With no capital outlay at all, I formed Wiester's Services in 1984. We worked with our personal vacuum cleaner, clothes, and less than $50.00 in cleaning supplies.

I would like to see money budgeted for a cleaning service in every household. I do not feel that having one's house serviced is a luxury. I believe it is a necessity people owe to themselves so that they will have more time to do what they enjoy. In addition to word-of-mouth, I placed a one-time-only advertisement in a community newspaper and received one reply. However, that one client is still with me six years later. As I became involved in my business, I talked and dreamed of starting a **real** company; a company with training programs, uniformed and supervised crews, Christmas bonuses and the like. Today our pink-jacketed staff and white CLEANY BOPPER vehicles can be seen throughout metropolitan Baltimore and surrounding counties. Our employees appreciate their benefit programs and anticipate the awards, bonuses, and yearly company events.

Like many other small business owners, I had to develop my own direction and make numerous decisions about my business. I could not rely on the expertise of a franchiser. We made many mistakes, but as they say, 'experience is the best teacher'. What I didn't know was you get the 'test first and the lesson later'. Some of these lessons were very expensive mistakes -- but we only made them once.

For example, at one time I did not know that a client's credit could be checked in advance of signing a contract. In addition, I didn't realize the importance of initials on contracts, and that one could ask for a 50% deposit up front to cover payroll and supplies. One of my early commercial contracts became part of a family litigation and I found myself facing the prospect of covering wages and benefits amounting to several thousand dollars. It was one of those times when I questioned the risk-taking and the learning process of a small business. Fortunately, we did receive payment, although it took almost a year and we received no interest. As a consequence, I did learn how to make accounts receivable calls -- which very quickly became another necessary business lesson!

On July 2, 1986, I incorporated CLEANY BOOPERS and set in place new plans to keep up with the growth I was experiencing. As president, I added additional services to support the residential cleaning. A workforce of twenty two, most of whom are full-time employees, wash windows, clean carpet and upholstery, strip and wax floors, clean post-construction housing, clean apartment complexes, and perform small-to-medium-sized office and retail store janitorial service. I desperately needed and hired an office manager; someone to keep me straight. One thing I learned was to never give your office manager a vacation in a one-person office!

As the business grew, I became involved in the National Association of Women Business Owners (NAWBO). This network of women provided support and valuable business information. The resources of NAWBO were important to me during these first critical years of business. I would encourage any woman business owner to join this wonderful association, not only for the camaraderie and support, but for all the guidance and direction in the business world.

The business developed the framework for growth. Our crews are available, trained, bonded and supplied with uniforms and equipment. Since two people work on a team, the job is completed and checked quickly, and a crew exits in a minimum of time. Special chores may be added to the routine cleaning, such as cleaning ovens, washing windows, polishing silver, preparing for move-ins or move-outs.

As I oversaw the growth of CLEANY BOPPERS, several challenges had to be met. I found that one of our main concerns was that many men bankers, accountants, and employees did not take women seriously. Many women use a low-key management style that emphasizes details, reason, and teamwork. Some male employees have learned to respond to more forceful approaches, such as swearing. They may ignore directives given quietly by a woman until retrained.

I found that women must be careful not to over extend the problem-solving, nurturing role with employees. Employees do have personal and job-related problems, but the woman business owner must keep everyone moving toward goals using the accepted procedures. For example, a woman can be more likely to excuse an employee's unwashed uniform if he or she has numerous problems. Yet, the image of the company is my responsibility. The line between concern for employees and the corporate good is a fine one.

With all the risks and problems involved, I saw a growing market for our services as more than fifty million women have entered the workforce, resulting in more money than time and energy. Women have little time to interview or train maids, buy cleaning supplies, or select the most efficient vacuum. To meet the business need, commercial expansion has already begun with radio ads and new accounts in the commercial division of the company. The need for thoroughly clean homes and businesses is one that CLEANY BOPPERS is determined to meet, and I plan to always have that vision!

If a woman has a skill or area of knowledge which meets the needs of our society today, she should take the risk of developing a small business. In addition to the financial rewards possible, the opportunity for both professional and personal growth is immense. With resources like NAWBO and U.S. Small Business Association, you will find that you are not alone in your quest for independence, security and personal growth. Women all around you extend a helping hand, share their expertise and encouragement. I took the risk! You can too!"

CLEANY BOPPERS, INC.
9319 Samoset Road, Randallstown, Maryland 21133
TEL: (301) 922-0018

NORA MULHOLLAND

THE OFFICE FURNITURE BROKER, INC.

Nora Mulholland formed The Office Furniture Broker, Inc. in 1982. Her Denver-based company deals in used furniture, offering companies a way to buy exactly what they are looking for at a savings available only on the secondary market. The initial operation started in Nora's bedroom with a portable showroom (a photo album of polaroid snapshots) and a 'Have Camera Will Travel' philosophy. After four years of hard work, her partner bailed out and left her with heavy debts. Not being a quitter, Nora continued to plod forward tenaciously against all odds. Today the company has 10 employees and a 10,000 square foot facility with an in-house inventory of nearly $2 million in products. They are now one of the oldest used office dealerships in the United States. Nora is past president of the Colorado Chapter of NAWBO, an active member of the greater Denver Chamber of Commerce, participates as an assistant in Dale Carnegie Training, the Leadership Denver class of '92, and the high school mentoring program of C.A.B.

Four years of hard work seemed to crumble, rather crash around us. The 'partner' that was to save the business was bailing out and the dreams were quickly turning into nightmares - again.

At one point, the 'It can't get any worse' theory got worse, as over $45,000 worth of unpaid, overdue bills were discovered. If that wasn't enough, our credit line was maxed, the data processing operator managed to wipe out the entire inventory data base, and sales were in a slump. Certainly anyone with enough sense should at least know when to quit. But, this owner was too scared to stop long enough to realize how deep the trouble really was and thus we continued to plod forward.

Our story starts out like many, fired for political reasons at the height of a fairly successful career, the idea of a repeat performance for another business enterprise did not seem too appealing. Thus, in November of 1982, The Office Furniture Broker (Inc. was added in 1984) was formed.

The concept was fairly simple in those days, find people or businesses with the need to sell existing excess office furniture and locate buyers for such and voila! - a deal is made. The showroom was portable and quite flexible, existing of a photo album of polaroid snap shots of various products. 'Have camera will travel', was the mode of operating for nearly the first two years.

The initial operations moved within the first three months from my bedroom to a spacious 700 square foot, subleased (from Drug Rehabilitation Center) office. Armed with a phone, an answering machine, my college typewriter and a few sparse pieces of furniture (on consignment, of course), the plunge to appear as a true business was made.

Employee number one was on board just long enough to witness a 'buyer' selling a truck load of furniture that we were representing to a third party, but he had omitted paying for the

174

product. The end of the chase scene, my Honda tailing the truck through downtown Denver, did result in the receipt of payment, but just short of getting slapped with a libel suit from the innocent third party.

In 1984 we were presented with a new set of challenges. My soon-to-become partner and I had been negotiating two separate large contracts, and to our wonderment, we were awarded both within hours of each other. Although exciting, the smaller of the two projects (150 offices worth) **had** to be out of the thirty second floor space within 72 hours and we had no warehouse!

Immediately we subleased 8,000 square feet from an organization that allowed us to set our desk and phone up, literally in the warehouse, on the cement dock. It wasn't until several months later that we were able to move into the office space of the building. Towards the end of the year, it became apparent that renegotiating the lease with that owner was not feasible, and we relocated to a 10,000 square foot facility that has housed our operation to date.

For the next two years we struggled along, added a warehouseman and an outside sales person, sales continued to grow slowly, cash flow seemed non existent and often it was questionable as to how long we could hang in there. Yet, during this time, we never had a lay off or missed a payroll, with the exception of myself.

1988-1989 became one of the most trying periods in the history of this organization. In summary, and not being one to relish reliving nightmares, our office manager and long time employee relocated to another state and her replacement was so over her head that it wasn't until she wiped out our $9,000.00 data base that she got my attention. After her termination the REAL problems like the unpaid debts were discovered, the custom software people we had contracted with went out of business, my 'partner' decided to throw in the towel and our credit line was maxed out. But, with the tenacity that is found in many entrepreneurs, we have managed to live through those years. As of today, we are 10 employees, and have been in our 10,000 square foot facility for over six years and are renegotiating to double our space. We also offer in-house computer aided design, have an extensive inventory of case goods and Herman Miller systems of over 3 million (inventory we now own vs. consign), and sold 1.2 million (equivalent of 4+ million in new furniture) last year.

Nearly nine years ago, the chatter of family and friends asking 'When is Nora going to get a real job'...still rings in my ears, and memories of lying awake nights and thinking of hocking diamond stud earrings only seem like yesterday.

We are fortunate. We've worked hard, have earned a solid reputation, developed a strong clientele, have reliable and trustworthy employees and are one of the oldest used office dealerships in the United States.

Yes, ignorance is bliss. For had I known then what I know now, I surely would have had enough sense to pass on this wonderful experience called entrepreneurship, but I guess we'll never know."

THE OFFICE FURNITURE BROKER, INC.
4905 Nome Street, Denver, CO 80239
TEL: (303) 371-4542, FAX: (303) 371-4540

PHYLLIS L. APELBAUM
ARROW MESSENGER SERVICE

Phyllis L. Apelbaum is the founder and president of Arrow Messenger Service, Inc., in Chicago. Phyllis' formal education ended with the eighth grade. She worked 22 years for a cab company and a messenger service. When her father died in 1972, she decided to use her $3500 inheritance to start her own company. After being refused a license to operate on 17 occasions, she won a battle with the Illinois Commerce Commission and opened her business. Today the company employs over 175 people, and has annual sales of over $4 million. Phyllis serves many professional, civic, and charitable organizations, feeling strongly the need to give something back to her community. Mayor Daley recently appointed her as Chairperson for the City of Chicago's Affirmative Action Advisory Board. In 1989 Phyllis was inducted into the Chicago Commission on Women Hall of Fame. In 1990, only she was surprised when President Bush presented her with an award as first runner-up U.S. Small Business Administration National Small Business Person of the Year.

"My story is not typical of what most people consider the usual road to success in business.....

My formal education ended after eighth grade, when it was necessary for me to leave school and help support my family. Today, I own a messenger service that is well respected in the industry, and does over $4 million annually.

As many women of my generation, I married young and had a child. Unfortunately, I also divorced at a young age, and was left to support my son alone. One thing I knew from my experiences working part time was that I truly enjoyed public contact, preferably in a fast paced environment, so I took a job at American United Cab Company as a telephone operator. Over the years I learned different aspects of the business, eventually moving into a dispatch position.

After 10 years at American, I left there to go to work at City Bonded Messenger Service, which no longer exists. It was a move that offered me greater opportunities, and I felt it was time to move on. Little did I realize when I started there how important that step would be to my entire future! The owners of the company were wonderful people, and from them I learned every aspect of the messenger business. They eventually sold the company, and I had somewhat of a personality clash with the new owners. After 12 years there, although I enjoyed the business, the job was not the same. I began to think of making a change.

It is ironic that a personal tragedy is what afforded me the opportunity to start my own business. When my father died in 1972, I was left with a $3500 inheritance. I decided that instead of going to work for someone else, it was time to start my own company. It was that money that funded the beginning of Arrow Messenger Service, Inc., on November 1, 1973.

At that time, no woman had every been granted an operating authority from the Illinois Commerce Commission, which governs our industry. Although I certainly had the necessary experience and knowledge to run a messenger service, I was refused a license to operate. Frustrated after 17 attempts, I went directly to the Commissioner and voiced my grievances with the commission. Unaware until then of my situation, he began investigating, and personally issued my license shortly thereafter.

When Arrow opened in 1973, we had an office at 333 N. Michigan Avenue, three walking messengers and two drivers. I had friends at two large companies who had supported me during my licensing hearings, and had agreed to give us a try, but two clients weren't going to keep me in business. I passed out leaflets advertising Arrow in our new building and the surrounding area. By the end of our first week in business we had approximately 25 clients. In fact, many of those original clients are people we're still serving, 18 years later. And I'm still selling our services, although I no longer pass out flyers door-to-door!

Starting up a business requires complete dedication, especially when things are tight financially. For years I worked from early in the morning until well past midnight, trying to keep on top of things. In those days it was not uncommon for me to sleep on the floor at the office - I was just too tired to go home, and I knew I had to be back before 6:00 a.m. The pride of ownership, and drive to succeed, though, were just too strong for me to give up. Little by little the company started to grow and I was able to hire staff people.

One of the reasons we have been successful and maintained an excellent reputation is our dedication to quality service. From the beginning, I have required that all couriers wear a complete uniform, which includes black pants, yellow shirt with an Arrow emblem, and a black tie. Any jackets or hats must be the ones chosen as part of the uniform. This may seem like a small detail, but it's a rule we strictly enforce. Our clients expect our couriers to present themselves professionally while delivering for them, and they do. All couriers are hired as employees of the company. The industry norm is to hire them as independent contractors. Although it costs substantially more to operate this way, it is important that we have that edge when it comes to attracting and retaining the best couriers in the business.

Our philosophy since the day we opened our doors has been that each client is equally important, no matter how large or small; and that each client deserves the quality service they have come to expect from Arrow. Our rates are set at a reasonable level for the marketplace, and all customers pay the same amount for service. I am well aware that many of my competitors start out with inflated rates and 'deal down' to an acceptable level, but that has never been our practice. It is sometimes difficult to convey that philosophy to prospective clients, but we feel strongly that to most people quality - not price - is the most important factor in choosing a service. Our consistent growth over the years, and high client retention rate, prove that we must be right.

Flexibility to client needs is crucial in any service business, and we consistently look for ways to better serve our clients. We are fully computerized, and we have an in-house programmer who is constantly working on updating and improving our programs. Our customers are contacted regularly to get feedback on our service, which we review to see where we might need to make changes. Additional services have been added as we've recognized a need for them, including next-flight-out air service, and on-site biker program, specialized routing service, and mail delivery service. Recently we opened a new division, Arrow Temporary Service, which specializes in mailroom clerks, photocopy and fax operators, shipping and receiving clerks, and similar temporary employees.

Arrow Messenger Service currently employs over 175 people, and this year will do over $4 million in sales. I still love what I do, after being in this business for over 30 years, and I can't imagine doing anything else for a living. One of the best things about reaching this point in my career, and having people around me whom I can trust to run my business, is the time I now have for other interests. I am involved in many professional, civic, and charitable organizations, and I feel very strongly the need to give something back to the community which allowed me to become a success.

Recently I was appointed by Mayor Daley as Chairperson for the City of Chicago's Affirmative Action Advisory Board. The board was created to administer certain aspects of the city's Minority and Women-Owned Business Enterprise Procurement Program Ordinance, commonly known as the Minority Set-Aside Program.

The Lakefront Single Room Occupancy Corporation (LFSRO) is one of the charitable organizations I have become involved with in recent years. Serving homeless and low-income Chicago men and women, the LFSRO purchases, renovates, furnishes and manages SRO's, providing social services for its building residents. We are currently nearing completion of our second residence.

For the third year in a row, I have the pleasure of serving as the Chairperson for the Annual Variety Club Children's Charity Carnival. This event provides a day at an actual carnival to over 2500 disabled and disadvantaged children who may never have a chance to enjoy the experience otherwise. In addition, all funds raised beyond the actual cost of the carnival are contributed to the Ann & Jack Sparberg Children's Limb Bank at the Rehabilitation Institute of Chicago. Obviously, this event is one that is particularly near and dear to me.

My business success, as well as contribution to these and other important organizations, has led to several awards, both civic and professional. While I am certainly proud of each and every honor I receive, there is one in particular I would like to mention.

In 1990 I was named the Illinois Small Business Person of the Year by the Small Business Administration, and each of the individual state winners were invited to Washington, D.C., to participate in the national awards. As I had never been to Washington, I decided it would be an interesting trip, although I was certain I had no chance of winning. To my surprise -and certainly pleasure - I was named the first runner-up nationally and was presented with my award by President Bush in the White House.

When I began working as a telephone operator at American Cab over 30 years ago, I had no thought of opening my own business. When I did open Arrow 18 years ago, I was worried about just keeping the doors open and paying the bills. Never did I even dream that I would one day be standing in the White House accepting an award from the President of the United States. I can only hope that the future remains as exciting as the past has been."

ARROW MESSENGER SERVICE
1322 W. Walton Street, Chicago, Illinois 60622
TEL: (312) 489-6691, FAX: (312) 489-6920

NADIA SEMCZUK
THE PARTY STAFF

Nadia Semczuk, at age 28, is a partner and President of The Party Staff and owner of its sister company, Los Angeles Professional Servers Company. The companies, with nearly 100 part-time employees, specialize in staffing and service consultation for the restaurant industry. Nadia is a native Californian with Soviet immigrant parents. She grew up in an environment that gave her little support or encouragement, especially toward female entrepreneurship. Despite having lived on her own since the age of sixteen, Nadia finished high school and put herself through college. After working in various service capacities for a number of years in the restaurant and hotel industry, she and a partner formed The Party Staff in 1987 in her apartment. Since then the company has moved to an office, gained support staff and experienced tremendous growth. Nadia is proud to have overcome the colossal obstacles she faced along the way.

"Dad, you can't treat your customers like that.....

Being a business woman is not all that easy and, in fact, being in business is not what I expected. But looking back at my life, I am so glad to be where I am.

I was the youngest child in my family and completely opposite from my brother and sister. From what my parents tell me, I had an answer for everything. I was stubborn, independent and always had to have my own way. I was always looking for ways to make money, so when the opportunity arose, I sold lemonade, cookies or my old personal belongings.

While growing up, my father started his own jewelry store and I used to hang out there on weekends. He is a Soviet immigrant and was used to old world customer service, which means the <u>owner</u> is always right. He would get mad at them for the smallest things, so I'd tell him, 'Dad, you can't treat your customers like that!' He would say, 'Don't tell me how to run my business! What do you know about how to handle customers?' He couldn't understand that his 11 year old daughter was already learning the value of good customer relations. Perhaps, if he would have listened to me, he may have succeeded in his own business. Even at that time, I knew that customers are everything and that if you did not treat them right you could not be successful.

When I was nine years old, my parents divorced and my home life fell apart. It drove me to move out when I was only 16. I was determined to be someone important some day and to have a happy family, unlike what I had experienced. At that point, I really had no direction in life. My parents had never encouraged me to do bigger and better things, and I never got any support from them. I knew that if I did not leave that negative environment behind, I would never accomplish anything. On my own, I supported myself through high school in Los Angeles, which was tough, so I grew up really fast. I didn't get along with anyone in school because no one could relate to me. But instead of letting it discourage me, I believe it strengthened my independence and individuality. I became

184

even more determined to become successful and show my classmates a thing or two. I managed to graduate -- no G.E.D. for me -- with an emphasis on business.

I knew college was the right direction, so off I went, with no money in my pocket. (My dad had squandered my college fund on his failing business.) I had two jobs while studying Video and Television production full time at Los Angeles Community College. I advanced myself to various positions in the entertainment field, including Assistant Director for USA Video Company. I also worked as a waitress, did free-lance photography, and sold hand decorated jewelry and T-shirts at swap meets on weekends. After a brief transfer to the University of California at Berkeley, I entered U.C.L.A. and landed a job with Merv Griffin Enterprises as a Client Hostess. At that point I really wanted to start my own business on the side.

At the time, my boyfriend was running an unsuccessful D.J. (Disc Jockey) service and was ready to give it up. I persuaded him to let me take over the advertising, bookings and customer service areas of the business and count me in as a partner. Because of his Italian machismo, he wasn't too keen at first, but after awhile he couldn't overlook the reason for his newfound success. The only problem that I had was that he took all of the credit and didn't pay me anything. We broke up and his business quickly faded away. The taste of business ownership didn't fade away for me, though, and I was determined more than ever to go it alone and get the recognition that I deserved.

Because of my past experience as a waitress, I started working for a small temporary food service staffing company. I worked various types of parties and events, as supervisor and server. After awhile, I realized that it would be a great business to have, on an even larger scale. I noticed the company I worked for wasn't providing quality service, since most of my co-workers knew virtually nothing about food service. I figured I could start my own company and do a better job. Although I knew little about running a business, I began focusing on this goal and saving capital.

In order to improve my service skills and knowledge, I got a job with the new J. W. Marriott in Century City, which was one of the flagship hotels of the chain. They were extremely concerned about the service, so I trained for two months and learned everything from A to Z. While working there, I also got a job with the Four Seasons in Beverly Hills, due to its world renowned reputation for service. I sometimes worked twelve hour days, seven days a week, but this met both my goals of gaining experience and saving money.

Finally, the day arrived when I was ready to take the leap and start my own business. I had met Brian Lillie at the temporary staffing company, and we shared the same ideas and philosophy on service standards. We decided to go into business together. At first I was a little hesitant because of my previous experience of being in business with a man, but Brian had no problem sharing the responsibilities and credit. We started in an apartment with fifteen staff and grew into an office after three months.

Starting the business was not an easy task. We did a lot of research and learned everything we could to keep the business going, including the importance of cash flow, customer relations, marketing and employee relations. In retrospect, I truly believe the most difficult time I had was in starting the business. I can't begin to describe the fears I went through, like if we'd have enough money to cover our expenses, if we'd have enough business to survive or if we could keep our standards up, not to mention a hundred things more.

I can remember waking up in a cold sweat every night, having butterflies in my stomach and being totally unsociable for months. It was not easy, but overcoming obstacles is one of the major satisfactions of owning a business. The challenges never go away, and as we grow, the business goes with me wherever I am, 24 hours a day. After two years, we now have one hundred part-time employees, have moved into bigger offices and have plans of expanding nationwide.

My life goals and dreams are coming true. I married my business partner, Brian, on April 14, 1991. We are a great team, although working together and being married is not that easy. It takes a lot of understanding and communication between us to keep a successful relationship in business and marriage. Brian is good with finances and also handles sales for the company. On the other hand, my strong points are in planning, customer relations, management, organization and food service. Our different strengths complement each other.

I am starting to really look forward to the future. I truly believe in our company and everything it stands for. We are very customer service oriented, charge a competitive and reasonable rate for our service, and offer quality. In order to diversify, yet complement our current business, I've recently started a sister company, Los Angeles Professional Servers School. It includes production of a series of service videos geared toward training employees of catering companies, restaurants or any other food service market. I am also planning to help charitable causes in the near future, because I feel that in being blessed, it is my duty to bless others.

When I look back at it all, I would do (most of it) again, even though at times things were really tough. There were moments when I thought I could never make it. I am now unashamedly proud of myself and what I have become. Being a business owner is a very satisfying lifestyle."

THE PARTY STAFF
8489 West Third St., Suite 1021, West Hollywood, CA 90048
TEL: (213) 653-8441

ELLEN LOCKERT & NINA JACKSON

LOCKERT-JACKSON AND ASSOCIATES, INC.

Nina Jackson (left in picture) and Ellen Lockert (right in picture) of Lockert-Jackson and Associates, Inc. in Winslow, Washington, are pioneering the new field of video publishing. With extensive experience in broadcast television, the women have created a unique video training service for emergency medical service personnel, providing reasonably priced broadcast quality video presented in a manner that entertains and enhances learning. The two partners' skills and experience complement each other perfectly. Nina, a pioneer woman in her field, has worked as an editor in television broadcasting since 1967 and is a firefighter/paramedic. Ellen directed and produced young people's programs for which she won two EMMYS. The partners met, saw a need and launched Emergency Medical Update in 1987 now producing training materials for 70,000 Emergency Medical Source providers worldwide. Theirs is the story of sheer stamina, a passionate belief in their project and the joy of having built a successful and **VITAL** business.

"Starting a business is _not_ for the faint of heart.....

When Nina Jackson and I met in 1983, we had combined experience of 30 years in broadcast television. We worked at KING-TV in Seattle. She was the Chief Editor in the News Department. I was a Producer with the 'Good Company Show', the morning talk show. We'd both had a lot of fun working in television and over dinner one night we discovered that we were also both ready to move on. What we didn't realize was that our skills and experience complemented each other perfectly.

Nina had come up the hard way. One of the groundbreaking generation of women in broadcast, she began work in Los Angeles in 1967 as an apprentice editor. She started in film, working at MGM, Paramount, 20th Century Fox and Hanna Barbera. Initially the work was hard to come by. It was on a project basis and, at that time, even the union was hesitant to support women in the field. Nina was often the first woman to enter a shop and learned early to parry innuendo and insult as she 'paid her dues'.

In 1971 Nina was hired by the KNBC News Department in Burbank, California. During the following years she edited news stories there while putting in hours of overtime for NBC Nightly News and the 'Today Show'. She was eventually hired full time for NBC and broke new ground as the first female editor on the West Coast. During this period she travelled extensively, covering such historic stories as the Vietnam War and the Patty Hearst kidnapping.

After seven years working in Los Angeles broadcast, Nina headed north for clearer skies and fresh air. Once there, she continued her career in television news, first at KOMO and later as Chief Editor at KING-TV. It was during this time that she became a volunteer firefighter/emergency medical technician in rural Snohomish County.

I was a late bloomer. With a BS in psychology under my belt, I spent my 20's exploring a variety of careers. It wasn't until I was 28 that I translated an interest in photography to

190

television production. A couple of semesters of video production at Bellevue Community College and a lot of luck landed me a position as floor director at KING-TV, the Seattle NBC affiliate.

Three years learning the broadcast television business as floor director and director trainee led to an opportunity to produce and host a science show for children. I got an EMMY for the program and went on to produce a teen magazine show that won a second EMMY and Action for Children's Television Award. Additional productions included talk shows and live remote programming.

I loved the people and the excitement of television. I also knew I wanted my own business. My dad was a successful entrepreneur who talked at length about the joys of ownership. I was 38 and I knew it was time to give it a try. My vision for a product came with clarity and undeniable force: a subscription training service that was both educational and entertaining.

About the same time, Nina was involved in providing emergency medical service (EMS) training for the Seattle Fire Department. She was appalled by the dreary slide shows and training videos. She could see that there was a need for a revolutionary change in the way training was delivered. And, she had just enough capital to begin development of an alternative.

The concept of monthly video training service for Emergency Medical Personnel felt like the right idea at the right time to both of us. Early market research reinforced our instincts and **Emergency Medical Update** was launched in November, 1987. Since we'd underestimated costs and neither of us had previous business experience, the learning curve was steep. Our passionate belief in the project and sheer stamina helped us work an endless stream of 14-16 hour days. 'Entrepreneurial terror' was a part of every one of those hours. We deferred pay as we built a team of smart, committed employees who believed in the mission and were willing to work long hours for nominal compensation. One of our corporate goals was to create a humane and nurturing work place that allowed each person to be their best. From this goal a corporate culture developed that was based on teamwork, collaboration and a sense of adventure.

A key member of the team arrived within the first few months. Marit Saltrones knew the concept was right and brought a whole range of invaluable skills to the emerging business. Her affinity for systems and data management skills created a solid and orderly base which supported the rapid growth of the first four years. As systems were installed, she moved into video production. This allowed me to move into sales and marketing and Nina to further her EMS education by training as a paramedic. Marit is current Senior Producer of the monthly program as well as a shareholder in the business.

As the business grew, an informal network of business advisors gave freely of their time and expertise. A local banker extended our first line of credit after larger banks turned us down. Attorneys, CEOs, marketing experts and bankers each donated hours of expertise and encouragement. People were eager to help!

For both of us, the focus of that first year was creating the best possible product and getting it to the market place. An 800 number was installed in our basement office and ads placed in a leading trade journal. Once each month's program was completed, we hit the road for yet another trade show. While response at trade shows was enthusiastic, the phone was not exactly ringing off the hook. It was time for more aggressive tactics. We acquired state lists of EMS provider agencies and hired people to call and offer previews of the program. For every six preview tapes sent, a subscription was sold. Over time, a telemarketing unit was born that now consists of six sales people and a supervisor.

We knew that eventually there would be competing products and we were right. Some of them have been overpriced and some poorly implemented. We think our success factors include a clear understanding of what the market needs...broadcast quality training at an affordable price plus a commitment to delight and amaze our customers with service and quality at every stage of our relationship.

Emergency Medical Update currently provides training for 70,000 EMS providers around the world. It is an approved source of continuing education in most states. Lockert-Jackson and Associates, Inc. is now developing a second product line. We envision a time when we'll produce a variety of services, each of which offers specialized training to different markets. The medium might be video tape, interactive video or satellite. The message will always be that learning can be fun.

While there have been hard times, there is an exhilaration to building a successful business unlike anything either of us has ever experienced. There is pride at creating something from nothing. There is intellectual stimulation solving problems and exploring opportunities. There is joy in creating a nurturing work place and satisfaction from providing a necessary and valuable service. However, starting a business is **not** for the faint of heart. You need to love what you're doing. It will take longer and cost more than you ever imagined. The costs will be physical and emotional as well as financial. Once you understand the costs, you need to be willing to pay the price. Do your homework. Know your market. Don't be afraid to ask for help. And, most important, be prepared to love your staff and customers to death. Without them, you're nothing."

LOCKERT-JACKSON AND ASSOCIATES, INC.
219 Madison Ave. So.
P. O. Box 11380, Winslow, WA 98110
TEL: (206) 842-9775, FAX: (206) 842-5640

EMILY H. MERRILL
BRYSTIE, INC.

Emily H. Merrill is the Chief Turtle of Brystie, Inc., a six million dollar wholesale/distribution company that sells cold weather accessories, hats, headbands and neckwarmers, under the labels of 'Turtle Fur' and 'Mountain Ladies & Ewe'. At 48 she was married to John W. Merrill who is now a partner in the business as Chief Financial Turtle. Emily graduated from a private high school in New York City then pursued a brief ski racing career. With some retail experience she opened a children's clothing store in Stowe, Vermont in 1971. On the ski slopes she recognized the potential of a friend's fleece neckwarmer as a marketable product. Brystie was opened and 'Turtle Fur' hit the marketplace in 1983. This past year 40,000 dozen neckwarmers sold and are now helping to keep America warm. Emily has always been involved in the community and with skiing. She currently serves on the Stowe Planning Commission, the Regional Industrial Development Council, the United States Ski Industries national trade show committee and is a director of the Helen Day Art Council. She was chosen as the Vermont Small Business Person of the year by the U.S. Small Business Administration and in addition was selected the Small Business Person for all of New England for 1991.

"Taking risks are not half so scary if you ask yourself, What do I have to lose?.....

To describe me, people might use words like creative, optimistic, competitive, a workaholic, energetic and committed to success. I don't know if those are classic traits of an entrepreneur but they have helped me. What they do not know is that sometimes I lie awake at night with worries and doubts. These are also probably entrepreneurial traits. My forte in the business is deciding on products that will sell and selling them. I absolutely love to sell and market my products. However, to make selling really easy I make sure that whatever Brystie sells is superior, original, more practical, a better price and/or has its very own niche. Essentially I am committed to making 'better mouse traps' and to telling the world about them.

After years of standing on ski slopes watching my children race I immediately recognized a fleece neckwarmer a friend showed me as being the best thing for skiers since the buckle boot. I had her make some for my children's store and told her that she should be marketing them. When after two years she had done nothing with the idea I found myself with extra space in the basement of my store, and I decided to market an improved model of her neckwarmer.

I started with one product, 'The Turtle's Neck', which is a very soft comfortable tube of fleece you can wear around your neck instead of a scarf. Instead of saying it was made with 100% acrylic fleece I said it was made with Turtle Fur, and made up the following story about it: '*We harvest Turtle Fur early in the spring from mock turtle's nests found on remote islands in Lake Champlain. It is spun by virgin acrilics to protect the turtles from the cold and the Wicked Itch of the North!*'

The 'Neck' was an instant success but on a very small scale. The first year reorders doubled the initial orders for a total of 300 dozen. Now we do over 40,000 dozen neckwarmers a year. It took two or three years for the 'Neck' to catch on and almost six years before it really started to dominate the ski market. We introduced additional products annually which also has

196

contributed to our rapid growth. I now look for growth with additional products and additional markets. This past year we bought out a related company adding nearly $400,000 to our gross sales for the year.

The right people are the key to successful growth. An entrepreneur is someone who creates a business, but it is not always someone who can run a business. I recognize my weakness as the latter and as hard as it was at first to delegate aspects of the business, I have entrusted it to some terrific people with whom I have good rapport, total communication and understanding, and mutual respect. One is my husband who joined Brystie in 1989. We make a great team because we have different skills and great mutual respect. The other key people reflect our commitment to quality, customer service and success, and as hard as it was at first to let go, we now let them do their jobs with trust and admiration.

Obviously financing an idea is crucial. During my years in the children's store business I was able to build up a relationship with a local bank. Though my education certainly did not cover any of these areas of study, basic education did teach me that good credit is invaluable. If you sign a loan be damn sure you have done your homework on how you plan to pay it off. If something changes your ability to pay, make sure the bank is the first to know, not the last, and they will probably help you work things out. Your loan agreement is essentially a partnership agreement and you should treat the lender like a partner by keeping him informed of the good and the bad.

Also important is what you call your business. When we applied for trade marks we were opposed by the Turtle Wax company for the use of the words 'The Turtle's Neck' and 'The Turtle's Top' with pictures of a turtle. I had been using them for a couple of years and when Turtle Wax opposed them it cost me close to $20,000 to fight them but I won. The Trademark office tends to help protect registered trademarks so it is up to the new person to prove why they should be allowed a mark. It can be a very expensive process and small companies are usually forced to back down. It is not as expensive to first choose a name for your company that is clear!

I have a bit of a pet peeve about Women in Business groups. They have their place and can be supportive but if you want to learn about business, as I am always trying to do, network with men and women business owners. It is somewhat reassuring that I have not yet met a man in business who has not worried about all the same things I worry about. Will the cash flow? How can I be sure I am making the right decisions? Can I really be responsible for all these people's welfare?, etc. etc.

I found it was also very important for me to learn about myself as a 'Woman Human Being'. I achieved this in co-ed self growth seminars and with counseling. They have both been exciting and positive learning experiences that have certainly helped me in every aspect of my life. There may be drawbacks to being a woman in business but I think the advantages may outweigh them. The most important thing I learned was that my parenting suffered not so much because of my commitment to work but rather a lack of commitment to parenting. Now I am a committed working parent who does not feel guilty and has become a good mother.

Taking risks are not half as scary if you ask yourself, 'What do I have to lose?', and then limit the downside and commit fully to success. I have figured that the worst that can happen to me is total failure, which would be a blow to my ego, an incredible learning experience, and leave me about where I started. It is definitely worth it and I encourage any one with a good idea to **'JUST DO IT'**."

BRYSTIE, INC.
192 Thomas Lane, P. O. Box 1535, Stowe, Vermont 05672
TEL: (802) 253-2191, FAX: (802) 253-7988

JACKIRAE SAGOUSPE

INTERNATIONAL DIVERSIFIED
TECHNOLOGIES, INC.

Jackirae Sagouspe is the co-founder of International Diversified Technologies, Inc. and IDT Seminars and Media located in Anaheim, California. IDT's market focus is to encourage and promote entrepreneurial concepts and small businesses in both the domestic and international marketplace. A former speech teacher, Jackirae arrived at her present business through a series of entrepreneurial ventures. She is now a recognized speaker on the topic of "International Entrepreneurism". She has carried that message into university classrooms, international business associations and in her own one-on-one consulting with American and foreign entrepreneurs. Jackirae has best been described as an "energizer" whose enthusiasm for business possibilities leaves no door of opportunity closed!

If you do not risk, you can not grow.
If you do not grow, you can not be your best.
If you are not your best, you can not be happy.
If you can not be happy, what else matters!

Dr. David Viscott

"I have often referred to myself as an 'entrepreneurial junkie'! My venture into entrepreneurship has been charted by a lifetime of 'messages' telling me to follow my own calling.

I have come full circle from my first steps into the business world. I am the co-owner of International Diversified Technologies, Inc., which my business partner, Bill Filbert, and I formed seven years ago to advise individuals and small companies in the electronics industry. As I promoted our business through speaking presentations and networking, I was intrigued by businesses with non-technical consumer products and services.

I soon found myself helping position, market and sell toys, microwaveable water bottles, crafts, language programs; and the list goes on. Most of my clients had great ideas but little money. Therefore, I literally became the 'market testing instrument' which meant it was 'show time'. I took the products to consumer and industry trade shows, fairs and expositions to gain feedback from target buyers. The 'ham' in me finally had a purpose!

I have taken these experiences and carved out a niche for myself as a professional speaker on the topic of working trade shows. We have created a new division of our company, IDT Seminars and Media, to market my seminars and video tapes focused on teaching one-on-one marketing and selling for the small entrepreneurial businesses. My first instructional video tape, 'Turning Your Trade Show Investment Into Profits' is being sold into the library system, through exhibition companies, to franchise organizations and directly to entrepreneurs entering the trade show arena. Every seminar presentation and video tape purchase generates networking with energetic and ingenious individuals who have decided to take

200

the plunge and go into business for themselves. I always advise people to follow their inner voice.

Personal risking was a message sent to me by my mother very early in life as an example of a woman who entered the working world of the first telephone operators and broke through the 'glass ceiling' of management during the 1930's. In the war years, while she shared the 'Rosie the Riveter' image, she did not exchange her skirt for overalls and a hard hat. With a seventh grade education and a drive to be the best she could be, she taught me to believe in myself regardless of the challenge before me. It was not a lesson I learned with a sense of awareness but rather through the world of (excuse the cliche) 'hard knocks'. Although my mother was a professional success story in her own right, the role she defined for me was: college was a must but marriage was not a necessity. It is important to note that she had not met the man who was to be my husband (now for twenty-one years); the man that has sent me positive messages and encouraged me at every new level of challenge I have desired to experience.

The last sentence is important in my story because my profile is not one of a success story in a single business but, rather that of an entrepreneurial roller coaster of experiences. Although I have enjoyed both the excitement of success in some ventures and disappointment in others, my message to all who read this is one of persistence and conviction to your inner voice and your perception of self fulfillment.

I began my professional life as a high school teacher instructing drama and English in schools serving multi-ethnic, primarily low income communities. The daily challenge was to create instruction that would hold their interest while teaching skills as well as important messages about life. I developed a course titled, 'Women in Literature and Society', which explored daily issues facing women through the reading of literature. The course was both popular and controversial. It attracted attention and a television program was produced by a local PBS station. This was my first taste of personal fulfillment based upon personal risk---it felt good and paved the way for my exit from education and entrance into the business world.

My career transition came at an interesting point in my life...I was reading Gail Sheeley's book Passages and turning thirty. I realized, if I was to be successful by my own definition, I was going to have to break away from the security of my teaching job and test my skills and talents in a new environment.

I took a battery of tests to diagnose my career potential. When they suggested that I apply for a job as an accountant, only I knew that Math had been a course I memorized but did not understand! Then I knew that only I could determine what I wanted 'to be'! I also realized that my inner voice continued to echo a need to be on my own...I wanted to create my own career path based on what I liked to do.

I think it is important to note here that I had quit trying to approach my career planning based upon either my education or past experience. I decided that, although I had never been trained or taken courses in selling and marketing, my natural talents and interests indicated that this would become the focus of my new career. My first test was marketing and selling myself doing what I loved most, 'public speaking'. I created a seminar called 'Tailoring the Voice of the American Business Woman'. After all, I had been a speech teacher for ten years and I was now a business woman...Voila!...instant credibility! The best part was I was getting paid to do what I did best -- speak. It was financially and personally rewarding.

My second entrepreneurial venture, which I conducted simultaneously with the seminars, was partnership in a start up business. We pioneered a new concept, that of video taping the contents of households and businesses for insurance identification purposes. He contributed the technical know-how behind the camera and I tackled the sales and marketing throughout all of Southern California. We were very successful in securing the support of insurance agencies and even a major department store chain. I learned a great deal about marketing and sales through experience and, unfortunately, I also learned that great entrepreneurial ideas do not always succeed regardless of how much money one pours into creative promotional materials. The real world included the 1982 recession and the fact that we had to educate our customers before we could sell them. We could not sustain the business under these conditions. Sadly, I had to take my new knowledge and debts and seek a new career opportunity.

I had always been told that when a door closes a window will open! My window was a brief stint of time in a straight commission sales job. The job description was simple: cold calling to prospect and kitchen table sales to generate income. I was successful but like a tight pair of shoes, the pain was too much.

At this point in time, I was approached by a group of investors beginning a management consulting firm to work with start-up technology companies in Orange County. The first company I consulted with was in the computer industry. It was the winter of 1983; the tail end of the 'boom era' in which engineers believed they could challenge big blue (IBM) and win. Entrepreneurism was 'in' and the American dream of instant wealth and fame was an industry fever. Unfortunately for many companies, and this included the one I was working with, the fever was linked with the germs of poor business management, financial irresponsibility and unrealistic goals for manufacturing, sales and marketing.

During the first quarter of 1984 we had sales in the United States and internationally for the two products that had reached the market and even for the promised new products...commonly called 'vapor ware'. While trying to coordinate the sales and marketing strategies of the company, I discovered that the company was in serious financial difficulties. Soon the only calls we were getting were from irate suppliers threatening legal action. The executives and engineers developed 'phone phobia' and my marketing challenge changed from pushing our product to defending our integrity.

Just as the brink of disaster looked destined, I met my current partner, Bill Filbert, who specialized in working with troubled companies in electronics. He agreed to help take on the challenge. We brought in new engineers, off loaded the manufacturing to subcontractors, fine tuned our purchasing to 'just in time' inventory control, and developed a consumer newsletter to open communication. Within six months, we were back on open account with most of our vendors. We introduced a total of seventeen products during a four year period. That real world experience surpassed any textbook or classroom lessons. I often refer to it as my 'Ph.D. in Business Survival'.

With the rapid change in technology our window of opportunity began to close. That is when Bill and I decided to put our expertise to good use and created International Diversified Technologies to help struggling companies hold fast to their growth potential. Our company has been very successful and everyday is exciting and challenging. As the cliche goes, we found that particular niche that was begging to be filled -- helping the small entrepreneurs to succeed in their segments of a giant marketplace!

I began my story with a quote that inspired me to take personal risk. I will close with a caption on a small painting that hangs over my desk, 'Challenges are simply opportunities with the wrapping still on!'"

INTERNATIONAL DIVERSIFIED TECHNOLOGIES, INC.
2211 Winston Road, Suite G, Anaheim, CA 92896
TEL: (714) 635-1815, FAX: (714) 635-9276

SHEILA RUDD

PRINT SHOP OF CHARLESTON, INC.

Sheila Rudd is the owner of Print Shop of Charleston, in Charleston, South Carolina. Sheila studied journalism in college and was employed by other small printing companies for a number of years, beginning with a part-time job while she was in high school. Hers is a small-business success story of a woman who was told that no female could open, operate, and sustain a printing business in the Charleston marketplace without a man to back her up. She opened her shop with a $3,500 loan from her mother, purchased used equipment and started her business in her garage. Her sole employee, a pressman who held a full time job during the day, would report to work after his other job; Sheila would feed him dinner and the two worked until late into the night. Sheila's business improved and she moved into a building. Then came Hurricane Hugo in 1989 and the building was destroyed and the equipment looted. With an SBA guaranteed loan Sheila relocated and her business has grown noticeably. Her story is an excellent example of the driving force and determination that have caused women in business to be such a hot topic for the 1990's.

"A woman can be just as good as a man in running her own business.....

I am honored to have been considered for publication in 'The Woman Entrepreneur' and delighted to submit the following article about me and my company, Print Shop of Charleston.

Before you read about the business which is my life and blood, I would like to share with you a little about myself, what drives me to do what I have been doing for a long time, and, if I dare be so presumptuous, to offer some advice about what it takes to make it in what many still consider a 'man's world'. As a very personal aside, one of the things that has driven me to succeed in my business was simply to make the important statement that a woman can make it also, and that she can be just as good as a man in running her own business. All I know for sure is that every day my doors are open for business, I feel good -- and that's good!

The printing industry is really all I know. Since it all started over 20 years ago as a part-time job when I was in high school, I have learned the trade by 'hands-on-training'. While employed by other small printing companies for a number of years, I became involved in practically every facet of the business operations - from typesetting to layout design, to production, supply inventory, to advertising, business office accounting and supervisory management. Along the way I completed two years of college, but the lure of the commercial printing industry caused me to discontinue college and take a higher position on a full-time basis in the job I was then doing. I became the 'heart and soul' main contributor to the profitability of the company and developed a reputation for quick work and quality. This, combined with a special brand of excellence in personalized service, kept customers coming back with repeat business and brought in new clientele as well as 'word-of-mouth' advertising.

First of all, I am nobody special. I am a small business success story that happened after a former boss (man) told me in 1979 that a woman could never open, operate and sustain a printing business in the Charleston marketplace without a man to back her up. A woman owning her own printing company was unheard of during this time. Most executive women worked in this industry for their husbands and only then they were considered 'owners'. But I had a dream of owning my own company and doing what I did best for myself instead of doing it for others' profit and benefit. I was making great money, the job had security, and I had gone up the ladder as high as I could go. But I was unsure, so I asked a friend who had been in the paper business to have lunch with me. At that time I asked him for his thoughts about my going out on my own. He explained that the industry looking down from the top was cutthroat and the competition would be too tough for a solely woman-owned enterprise. This was even better than I expected. It was a dare and challenge for me to undertake.

So in 1979 I made that dream begin--I quit my job and started Print Shop of Charleston. In the beginning I operated out of my mother's garage with one press, stone-age darkroom equipment, and the support of my family. I knew nothing about business management, but I did know the production part. During the day I sold the jobs, late afternoon I did all the camera work and early evening I cleaned the press, inked it up and got the plates ready for the part-time pressman I had hired to work 3 hours each night. Along with all of this I had a 3 year old baby that needed attending, a husband to convince I was doing the right thing and a mother to show that the $3,500.00 she loaned me for my dream was going to WORK!!!

Somehow I persevered the many long days and many short nights in growing the business from a modest operation into one of the top printing companies in the area today. The business was like giving birth to another child and helping nurture it into a life-long commercial printing company.

I felt many times like throwing up my hands and quitting because of several difficulties. After 5 months of operating in the garage, I had my eye on a small particular place to move, but it was owned by an elderly man who said, 'no way' after he met me. He said that he could not let me sign a lease because a printing company could not survive with only a woman owning it. Plus, he added, I was 'too, too young to do such a thing...' It was hard but fun to convince him that I was going to do it with or without his building. Five years later he congratulated me on such a well-run company.

The second difficulty of that same year came when I found out I was pregnant with my second child. I was already open with a full-time pressman, one saleswoman, myself, and again my supporting family. After a difficult delivery I was instructed to stay out of work for at least 6 weeks, but this could not be done. The business was only one year old, having financial problems and no capital backup. I went back to my mother and again asked for support. She loaned me $5,000.00. The baby became a part of the company and while I rocked her with one foot on the cradle on the floor of my office, I continued to work on the growth of Print Shop of Charleston.

In 1984 I became pregnant with my third child. I was happy and because the company was stable, I found time to enjoy her. Four months into the pregnancy I had an accident that put me into a back brace for two months. Finally in March I had another healthy baby girl, but during the next several months she developed breathing problems and was required to be monitored for six months by the Medical University of South Carolina Hospital. She recovered fantastically but again one week before her third birthday, she was severely burned from the neck down to the waist. I took off two weeks to be with her and was only able to work at night. My family was very supportive during these times and without them I would have given up by now!

In spite of all the personal and business start-up problems, I was here in my dream, an owner-operator of a new business finding out quickly that being a boss can get lonely, and that there was no boss to whom I could take my problems. In time, however, I developed a management support team which consisted of three important people: my banker, my accountant, and my lawyer. I consulted them on any major decisions, but basically I was on my own and learning very slowly how things were suppose to work.

208

The business had become more of a challenge. I knew I had to 'pay my dues' and my customers knew I had that 'whatever it takes' work ethic to give them what they wanted, when they wanted it. I never compromised in this area of quality personalized service. For ten years I struggled to provide a company worth being proud of.

Late in September of 1989, Hurricane Hugo blew away 85% of all that I had done. I managed to keep the business alive from a split location and then from a makeshift building until I could get my senses back to what really could be done. I was determined to bounce back no matter what it took and I doubled up on my efforts. With the support from many people who had believed in me and had been with me through the trials and tribulations of previous growing pains, I somehow managed to make it all stay together. I contacted the Small Business Administration Office and devised a business plan to secure funds for a new facility and to replace the equipment, supplies and whatever else I needed to recreate Print Shop of Charleston.

Today, Print Shop of Charleston is a full-service commercial printing company, and that 'whatever it takes' brand of personalized service sets us apart from our competition and brings us a large volume of repeat business. I feel that I am the driving force that makes it all happen. I also have created the staff that was needed to make the atmosphere that I so dreamed of. Without the support of my family, the qualified and loyalty of my employees, and the continuing customers, Print Shop of Charleston would not be possible.

There is a footnote to this woman-owned small business success story. My contagious enthusiasm has already spread to my three daughters and because of our growth and development, I have now opened another small business, MBT Enterprises, which produces children's educational coloring books. I try to divide my time between my girls and businesses in order that they too will become successful women entrepreneurs.

Would I do it again? You bet. I thrive in my environment and cannot see myself working for somebody else in this industry.

I take great pride in making a difference. In these times, helping others to see how they can become what they want to be is what I like to do. To be a successful business person it takes talent, energy, desires and the overall idea of not settling for second best because if you do, you'll be sure to get it!."

PRINT SHOP OF CHARLESTON, INC.
1045 Wappoo Road, Charleston, S.C. 29407
TEL: (803) 571-4811/4911, FAX: (803) 571-7270

PART III

Starting Your Own Business

RESOURCE DIRECTORY

HOW TO EXPLORE
BUSINESS OWNERSHIP

It's safe to say that everyone of us has, at some time, had a dream of owning a business. We all have ideas for creating new products, adapting existing products, or developing service businesses. Often, these ideas never quite make it out of our minds and into the marketplace. The profiles presented in this book are interesting and inspiring. They tell the stories of women who have realized their dreams by setting goals and by working toward those goals with dedication and determination. While reading this book you may have started to think about the possibility of developing your own business. As authors and business consultants, we would be remiss if we did not continue this presentation on entrepreneurship with information to aid you in exploring business ownership. First we will look into finding a business.

IDENTIFYING YOUR SKILLS
AND INTERESTS

It is important to identify the skills and interests you possess which can be turned into a business. Skills are abilities to use your knowledge proficiently. Interests are those things which you enjoy doing and which bring you pleasure. We would like to suggest that you place extra emphasis on the interest area, as you will be spending a great deal of time in your business pursuit and you might as well enjoy it. The ability to do well at your business may prove to be rewarding while the business is new, but if you do not like your work, it soon becomes a drudgery. Instead of looking forward to beginning your business day, you will be searching for a way to escape to a more interesting occupation.

If you are currently employed by someone else and enjoy what you are doing, could you develop an independent business? Beverly Duran developed Carretas, the Cart Company as an outgrowth of working for a pushcart vendor. After working for

22 years for a cab company and messenger service, Phyllis Apelbaum started Arrow Messenger Service. Perhaps you could work as an independent contractor and provide a service for other companies. Good examples would be financial management, accounting services, payroll services, computer programming, and technical writing.

Look at your hobbies and leisure time activities. Do they lend themselves to a business enterprise? Marty Maschino is a perfect example of turning one's hobby into a business. Her business, Attic Babies, began with craft show sales and grew into a doll manufacturing company which produces 9,000 dolls per week. Stephanie Slavin's love of flying helicopters led her to develop Aviation Business Consultants, Inc. If you enjoy traveling, have a knowledge of geography, and are skilled in writing, consider starting a travel service. Writing travel articles for magazines and newspapers, publishing guide books and newsletters, and developing a catalog of travel-related items could be business options. Perhaps you could teach or consult in your area of interest.

Often home equipment can be put to use. Bettye Smith started her business career by teaching typing in her kitchen. Her home-based business expanded and developed into the Alaska Business College. Your home computer could be used to develop a computer-related service business. Video recording equipment could be used in a service business which provides video recordings of special events such as weddings, business meetings, or athletic games. Audio taping and duplicating equipment may be used to record seminars and workshops for later duplication and sale.

Remember the old adage, "find a need and fill it". As one of the first black actresses to be contracted on a national television show, Vera Moore found a need for cosmetics for the ethnic market. She founded Vera Moore Cosmetics and developed a line of skin care and cosmetic products.

You may wish to explore a completely new area of interest. Take classes, apprentice, or work in the new area before developing your business. For example, if you are interested in catering, work in a restaurant part-time in order to get your "business education". You will learn about food handling, employee and customer relations, health codes and permits, and ordering of supplies. You will also be able to see if you really do enjoy working with food. When entering a new area of interest, it is better to keep your current job if possible and "moonlight" in the new field. This will give you the opportunity to research the new business while you still have a primary source of income. The additional money earned through your moonlighting effort can be set aside to start your own business.

We hear the term "networking" often. It is the exchange of experiences, advice, ideas, and information that takes place every day of our lives. Joining trade and professional associations, subscribing to trade journals and attending trade shows can give you access to people and to information which can help you develop your business. Lynda Milligan and Nancy Smith met at a quilting symposium. Their exchange of ideas led to the creation of their business, The Great American Quilt Factory, Inc.

DEVELOP A BUSINESS PLAN

Getting an idea for a business is just the start. Where do you go from here? It is best to determine if there is really a need for what you are proposing before a great deal of time and money is invested in the business. It is wise to develop a business plan. This is a feasibility study involving the examination of the steps involved in physically setting up the business and producing a product or providing a service, the development of a marketing plan, and the analysis of the costs involved in conducting a business.

WHERE TO FIND INFORMATION
The information you need to research and run your business effectively can be found through the resources of public, corporate, or university libraries, in governmental agencies, and in civic organizations. One of our under-utilized resources is the public library. The reference librarian in the business section can direct you to the materials you need.

Think through the business process. Some of the questions you may have are:

1. How do I physically set up a new business?

2. Is there a market for what I am proposing?

3. What permits or licenses will I need?

4. What types of legal structure would be best for my situation? How much competition is out there, where are they located, and how are they doing?

5. How do I find trade and professional associations for networking?

6. Where are my sources of supply?

7. What are the financial projections for my industry?

8. What are my possible sources of funding?

9. Where can I get the education that will help me with my business?

Take some time to write out your questions. Getting the answers will involve reading books, newsletters, and periodicals on the subject of your business. You will contact Trade and Professional Associations to get information on trade shows, industry trends, and sources of supply. Attendance and participation at meetings of civic organizations such as the Chamber of Commerce and professional organizations such as the National Association of Women Business Owners (NAWBO) provide opportunities for networking. Governmental departments issue publications containing statistical data and projections for their areas of concern. The Internal Revenue Service, Department of Commerce, and the Small Business Administration offer low cost classes concerning business development. Many colleges and community service programs now offer classes and seminars on business issues. The following reference section will help you locate resources which can provide the answers to your questions.

216

RESOURCE DIRECTORY

LIBRARY RESOURCES:

Bacon's Publicity Checker: Lists media as source of publicity information.

Encyclopedia of Associations: Lists trade and professional associations throughout the United States. Many publish newsletters and provide marketing information. These associations can help business owners keep up with the latest industry developments.

Encyclopedia of Business Information Sources: Lists handbooks, periodicals, directories, trade associations, and more for over 1200 specific industries and business subjects. Start here to search for information on your particular business.

U.S. Industrial Outlook: Provides an overview, forecasts and short profiles for 200 American industries, including statistics on recent trends and a five-year outlook.

Reference Book for World Traders: This three volume set lists banks, chambers of commerce, customs, marketing organizations, invoicing procedures, and more for 185 foreign markets. Sections on export planning, financing, shipping, laws, and tariffs are also included, with a directory of helpful government agencies.

Incubators for Small Business: Lists over 170 state government offices and incubators that offer financial and technical aid to new small businesses.

Small Business Sourcebook: a good starting place for finding consultants, educational institutions, governmental agencies offering assistance; specific information sources for over 140 types of businesses.

Sourcebook for Franchise Opportunities: Provides annual directory information for U.S. franchises, and data for investment requirements, royalty and advertising fees, services furnished by the franchiser, projected growth rates, and locations where franchises are licensed to operate.

National Trade and Professional Associations of the U.S.: Trade and Professional Associations are indexed by association, geographic region, subject, and budget.

INDEXES TO PERIODICALS & MAGAZINE ARTICLES:
These references can be found in the library. Periodicals and articles can be researched by subject. Become familiar with periodicals and read articles which contain information specific to your type of business.

Business Periodicals Index: an index to articles published in 300 business oriented periodicals.

Gale Directory of Publications: lists periodicals and newsletters.

Magazines for Libraries: directory of publications.

New York Times Index: a guide to articles published in the New York Times.

Reader's Guide to Periodical Literature: an index to articles published in 200 popular magazines.

Ulrich's International Periodicals Directory: lists over 100,000 magazines, newsletters, newspapers, journals, and other periodicals in 554 subject areas.

U.S. GOVERNMENT DEPARTMENTS:

You should also gather information from governmental agencies on your state and local level. The phone numbers given are for a central office. You can be directed to the department which can meet your specific needs. Ask to be put on a mailing list for appropriate materials. Most departments issue a catalog for their publications.

Bureau of Consumer Protection
Division of Special Statutes
6th and Pennsylvania Avenue NW
Washington, DC 20580

Consumer Products Safety Commission
Bureau of Compliance
5401 Westbard Avenue
Bethesda, MD 20207

Department of Agriculture
14th Street and Independence Avenue SW
Washington, DC 20250
(202)447-2791
Scope of this office includes food safety and inspection, nutrition, veterinary medicine, consumer affairs.

Department of Commerce
14th Street and Constitution Avenue NW
Washington, DC 20230
(202)377-2000
Department covers subjects of engineering standards, imports and exports, minority-owned business, patents and trademarks, business outlook analyses, economic and demographic statistics.

Department of Defense
The Pentagon
Washington, DC 20301
(202)545-6700
Covers mapping, nuclear operations and technology, foreign country security and atomic energy.

Department of Education
400 Maryland Avenue SW
Washington, DC 20202
(202)732-3366

Scope includes bilingual and adult education, libraries, special education, educational statistics.

Department of Energy
Forrestal Building
1000 Independence Avenue SW
Washington, DC 20585
(202)586-5000

Areas covered are conservation, inventions, fusion and nuclear energy, coal, gas, shale, and oil.

Department of Health and Human Services
200 Independence Avenue SW
Washington, DC 20201
(202)245-7000

Information available on diseases, drug abuse and research, family planning, food safety, occupational safety, statistical data.

Department of Housing and Urban Development
451 7th Street SW
Washington, DC 20410
(202)755-5111

Scope involves fair housing, energy conservation, urban studies, and elderly housing.

Department of the Interior
18th and C Streets NW
Washington, DC 20240
(202)343-7220

Covers the areas of water, natural resources, mapping, geology, fish and wildlife.

More Government Offices next page...

Department of Justice
10th Street and Constitution Avenue NW
Washington, DC 20530
(202)633-2000

Concerned with civil rights, drug enforcement, prisons, antitrust, justice statistics.

Department of Labor
200 Constitution Avenue NW
Washington, DC 20210
(202)523-6666

Divisions are concerned with labor-management relations, labor statistics, occupational safety and health, women's employment issues, productivity and technology.

Department of State
2201 C Street NW
Washington, DC 20520
(202)647-4000

Covers international affairs involving diplomacy, arms, drugs, human rights.

Department of Transportation
400 7th Street SW
Washington, DC 20590
(202)366-4000

Scope includes aviation, automobile, boat, rail, and highway standards and safety.

Department of the Treasury
15th Street and Pennsylvania Avenue NW
Washington, DC 20220

Covers the areas of customs, taxpayer assistance, currency research, development and production.

Environmental Protection Agency Protection Agency
401 M Street SW
Washington, DC 20460
(202)382-2090

More Government Offices next page...

Federal Communications Commission (FCC)
1919 M Street NW
Washington, DC 20554
(202)632-7000

Federal Trade Commission
Pennsylvania Avenue and 6th Street NW
Washington, DC 20580
(202)326-2000

Food and Drug Administration
5600 Fishers Lane
Rockville, MD 20857

U.S. International Trade Commission
500 E Street SW
Washington, DC 20436

U.S. Small Business Administration
1441 L Street NW
Washington, DC 20416
Scope covers minority and women's businesses, statistical data, export information, financial and management assistance.

BOOKS & PUBLICATIONS FOR THE ENTREPRENEUR:

Bobrow, Edwin. *Pioneering New Products: A Market Survival Guide,* Dow Jones-Irwin, 1987.

Breen, George and A. A. Blankenship. *Do it Yourself Marketing Research,* McGraw-Hill, 1982.

Clifford, Denis and Ralph Warner. *The Partnership Book,* Nolo Press, 1989.

Colman, Bob. *Small Business Survival Guide,* W.W. Norton,1987

DuBoff, Leonard. *The Law (in Plain English) for Small Business,* Madrona Publications, 1987.

Hawkin, Paul. *Growing a Business,* Simon and Schuster, 1987.

Holtz, Herman. *Advice, a High Profit Business,* Prentice-Hall, 1986.

Husch, Tony and Linda Foust. *That's a Great Idea,* Gravity Press, 1986.

Lavin, Michael. *Business Information: How to Find It, How to Use It,* Oryx Press, 1987.

Levinson, Jay Conrad. *Guerrilla Marketing: Secrets for Making Big Profits from your Small Business,* Houghton-Mifflin, 1984.

Mathewson, G. Bradley. *Asking for Money: the Entrepreneur's Guide to the Financing Process,* Financial Systems Associates, 1989.

Moran, Peg. *Invest in Yourself: a Woman's Guide to Starting Her Own Business.* Doubleday, 1984.

Ogilvy, David. *Ogilvy on Advertising,* Crown Publishers, 1983.

Pinson, Linda and Jerry Jinnett. *Anatomy of a Business Plan,* Out of Your Mind...and Into the Marketplace, 1989. **Note:** Business plan software for IBM and compatibles is also available from publisher, *Automate Your Business Plan,* 1991.

Pinson, Linda and Jerry Jinnett. *Marketing: Researching & Reaching your Target Market,* Out of Your Mind...and Into the Marketplace, 1988.

Pinson, Linda and Jerry Jinnett. *Out of Your Mind and Into the Marketplace,* Out of Your Mind..Into the Marketplace, 1988.

Pinson, Linda and Jerry Jinnett. *Recordkeeping: the Secret to Growth & Profit,* Out of Your Mind...and Into the Marketplace, 1988.

Pinson, Linda and Jerry Jinnett. *The Home-Based Entrepreneur,* Out of Your Mind...and Into the Marketplace, 1989.

Snowdon, Sondra. *The Global Edge: How Your Company Can Win in the International Marketplace,* Simon and Schuster, 1986.

Wilkens, Joanne. *Her Own Business: Success Secrets of Entrepreneurial Women,* McGraw-Hill, 1987.

Worthington, Anita and Robert E. *Staffing a Small Business: Hiring, Compensating, and Evaluating,* Oasis Books, 1987.

Doing Business In...(various foreign countries). Price Waterhouse Information Guides.

MAGAZINES:

> *Entrepreneur Magazine*
> *Entrepreneurial Woman Magazine*
> *Home Office Computing Magazine*
> *Inc. Magazine*
> *Nation's Business*

ORGANIZATIONS & ASSOCIATIONS

American Management Association
135 West 50th Street
New York, NY 10020
(212)586-8100

Offers management assistance, including home-study courses on audio-cassette.

American Marketing Association
250 S. Wacker Drive, Suite 200
Chicago, IL 60606
(312)648-0536

Publishes annotated bibliographies on important marketing topics, conducts seminars and other educational programs.

National Federation of Independent Business
150 W. 20th Avenue
San Mateo, CA 94403
(415)341-7441
      or
600 Maryland Ave. S.W., Suite 700
Washington, DC 20024
(202)554-9000

Represents small business interests to state and federal governments, distributes educational information and publications, and holds conferences.

Association of Collegiate Entrepreneurs (ACE)
Young Entrepreneurs Organization (YEO)
Center for Entrepreneurship
Box 147
Wichita State University
Wichita, KS 67208
(316)689-3000

ACE members are student entrepreneurs, while YEO offers membership to non-student entrepreneurs under the age of 30. Hold regional and national conferences, publish a newsletter, and act as information clearing house for young entrepreneurs.

National Association of Women Business Owners (NAWBO)
600 South Federal Street, Suite 400
Chicago, IL 60605
(312)922-0465

Helps broaden opportunities for women business owners by offering monthly chapter meetings, workshops and seminars, providing information and referral services to members, and maintaining a databank of women-owned businesses. Very strong national organization offering opportunities for getting involved in impacting legislation and working in the international marketplace.

International Council for Small Business
U.S. Association for Small Business and Entrepreneurs
905 University Avenue, Room 203
Madison, WI 53715
(608)262-9982

Professional organization for educators and entrepreneurs interested in the development of small business.

NATIONAL TRADE ASSOCIATIONS:

American Business Women's Association
9100 Ward Parkway
Kansas City, MO 64114
(816)361-6621

National Association for Female Executives, Inc.
127 West 24th Street
New York, NY 10011
(212)645-0770

National Association of Women in Construction
327 South Adam Street
Fort Worth, TX 76104
(817)877-5551

National Assocociation of Women Business Owners
See previous page

National Fed. of Business & Professional Women's Clubs
2012 Massachusetts Ave. NW
Washington, DC 20036
(202)393-5257

Roundtable for Women in Food Services
425 Central Park West,
New York, NY 10025
(212)865-8100

Women Construction Owners & Executives
P.O. Box 883034
San Francisco, CA 94188
(415)467-2140

Independent Computer Consultants Association
933 Gardenview Office Parkway
St. Louis MO 63141
(314)997-4633

LINDA PINSON & JERRY JINNETT

OUT OF YOUR MIND...
AND INTO THE MARKETPLACE™

Jerry Jinnett and Linda Pinson, the Small Business Administration's district and regional winner of the title Advocate of Women in Business 1991, are authors, speakers and consultants. The two are partners in a publishing company called Out of Your Mind...and Into the Marketplace™ based in Tustin, California. They have co-authored and published five business books (this is the sixth) and developed a business planning software program. In 1989, Jerry and Linda were named "Small Press Publisher of the Year". The U.S. Small Business Administration recently selected them to write their official business plan publication based on their book, "Anatomy of a Business Plan". Their books are in libraries and bookstores throughout the United States and are being used as textbooks and reference materials by universities, colleges, and economic development agencies. Linda and Jerry are well-known for their step-by-step business seminars which they present in colleges and at conferences throughout the United States. The following story is an attempt to see if the authors can do as good a job at profiling themselves as the rest of the women entrepreneurs who shared their stories with you in this book!

"Dare to value your thoughts, dare to write, and dare to let the public judge the worth of your words.....

Jerry and I are two small-town girls who were raised in the northern Nevada cattle communities of Lovelock and Winnemucca. We met in 1957 at Grand Assembly, the state convention for the Order of Rainbow for Girls. The kindred spirits in us (two mischievous natures) made for an immediate friendship that has only deepened with time. Jerry went on to nurses' training in San Francisco and I got my B.S. in Education from the University of Nevada in Reno. Shortly after school Jerry married an engineer and I was married to a Marine helicopter pilot. I was her maid of honor and she was my matron of honor. For 22 years we went our separate ways and raised our families. Phone lines remained hot, however, and at least once a year the two families spent a few days together. Most of the reunions occurred over New Year's Eve and the two of us were known for donning crazy costumes, getting on roofs, and embarrassing our children and husbands.

Finally in early 1985 Jerry's husband, who works for Bechtel, was sent to Orange County and for the first time we lived within commuting distance of each other. Jerry already had a business, Sunshine Art Products, dealing in stained glass and pressed flower giftware. My husband and I had a clock shop which I had started a year before he retired from the Marine Corps, so I was very busy being a clock repair lady. The businesses were successful and we were both working fulltime.

I can't give you a good reason why, but something made us both think that we needed to be in business together. While researching an idea we attended a large women's conference. Before the end of the conference, we had discovered that small business how-to information was hard to come by. There was a lot of hype, but not too much how-to. As a result, Jerry turned to me in the hallway between workshops and said, 'I was thinking that we could teach business classes and do a better job than most of these people.' I can't explain my reaction better than to say that I was feeling that 'great minds

230

think in the same track'. Two days later, Jerry and I made several appointments at the Community Colleges and succeeded in getting jobs teaching small business startup. We had a single class that we entitled 'Out of Your Mind...and Into the Marketplace'. Our entire business plan was to spend our time together doing something we liked. We planned to teach one subject and do it on a part-time basis. Being business partners, we also needed a name for our business--so we shrewdly also called it 'Out of Your Mind...and Into the Marketplace'. We teach all of our clients to be careful when naming their businesses. Our advice is not to use either a long or cutesy name. Obviously we did not practice what we preach!

Jerry and I were teaching this class for only a short time before it became obvious that students were clamoring for material to be written down for them to take home and use. How many of you have ever gone to a workshop and spent the time furiously writing down all the points that you thought might help you later on? Usually, everything goes too fast and you end up with scribbles and question marks.

Being entrepreneurs--and women who love a new challenge--a lightbulb came on. Why not write a step-by-step book to help people get through the logical steps to business start-up? And why not call that book **Out of Your Mind...and Into the Marketplace?** We did write it. Now we needed to find out how to sell it. What better way than to speak at a conference on the subject. It was time for another women's conference in Orange Co. and it was anticipated that 14,000 women would attend. We called their headquarters and presented ourselves as authors of a book. Instant credibility! We were asked to speak--on business planning? This was not exactly what we had envisioned. Steps to start-up were one thing, but business planning was another. We had both attended several business plan lectures and still did not understand how to write one, let alone teach someone else how to do it. However, the taste of fame was in our mouths and a simple 'yes' would put us at a podium in front of several hundred people. We did say 'yes' and then had a major case of wanting to take a long walk off of a short pier. We had three months to put up or shut up.

Not being the shut up type, we started some extensive research into the business planning process and came up with a format that would be approachable for the writer and acceptable to the lender. With all this work behind us, why not write a book on the subject--and why not have the first edition to sell at an exhibit booth at the conference? We wrote it, copied it on a Kodak copier, and bound copies in our hotel room the night before the conference. The next day we gave a seminar and sold books like crazy. We had become sudden experts to these people because we had written books and because we stood at a podium in front of them. What no one knew was that the only thing that kept them from seeing our knees shake was the podium that covered everything but our upper bodies.

From that point, we developed classes in marketing, accounting, pricing/costing, and business planning. We tested our materials on our students, researched in libraries and turned our findings into books on each of the areas. Now we have even managed to break into the computer field with the development of our business plan software.

It has often been said that 'writing is an art', but 'publishing is a business'. The writer is just that, the person who puts the words on a piece of paper, nothing more and nothing less. The publisher is the entity that does everything else. The publisher turns the manuscript into a finished work--refines the manuscript, designs the finished piece, prints it, pays for it and, more importantly, has the responsibility to market the work to the target audience. The 'writer' must be inspired. The publisher turns the inspiration into a business. When you write an article or a book, then, you will have to decide which of these responsibilities you want to accept...writer, publisher, or both.

With the same boldness (or naivety), we decided that we would now be publishers. Fortunately, Jerry and I have the perfect partnership. Our talents are complimentary and do not overlap in the wrong places. She is our marketing expert, proficient and adept at using the library. I deal in the financial aspects of our business and do all of our graphics. I don't darken the doors of the library except under duress and faithfully read all of the materials she so diligently highlights for me. I bow to her marketing decisions and she lets me keep us out of hock. Much to our own surprise, we must have done a good job because in 1989 we were named 'Small Press Publisher of the Year', an exciting moment for a pair of small town girls from Nevada.

Through lots of hard work and the same amount of good fortune, we have been able to get our books into the libraries and bookstores. Some are being used as textbooks in universities and colleges. This year we were honored when the U.S. Small Business Administration in Washington D.C. asked us to write their official business plan publication entitled 'How to Write a Business Plan'. We are certainly not famous, but we have established a niche in the marketplace as authors, publishers, and speakers. How could the authors of six books not know what they are talking about? In the last year alone, we have been paid substantial fees to present programs in San Francisco, Portland, Chicago, Pensacola, Anaheim, and Los Angeles, and York, Pennsylvania. We have been guest experts on several radio and television programs, and last month I was given the honor of being named SBA District and Regional Advocate for Women in Business, an award earned by both of us, but given to me due to logistics.

The point of all of this talk about Jerry and me is **not** to tell you how wonderful we are. It is to point out that our visibility has been multiplied one-hundred-fold because of the media of writing. There are thousands of wonderful teachers in our schools. We are not necessarily better teachers. You might say that we have been able to make ourselves more visible to our target market. Whatever your business is, you can enhance it and create additional visibility by putting your expertise on a piece of paper.

Publishing is serious business and requires lots of diligence and a mountain of work. We have both worked in business for many years and felt successful and rewarded in many ways. But in our wildest imagination, we never expected to experience the feelings that have emerged because of writing and publishing books. We never dreamed that the words that we set down on paper in our dining rooms could impact someone else's life and the success of their business. We did not know that we would someday walk into bookstores or libraries and see the fruits of our labor...or that we would answer our phones and consult with someone in London or Puerto Rico...or that we would have our book chosen as a Publisher's Clearinghouse Book Club Selection...or that we would be invited to speak at a major event...or that we would be called by the SBA in Washington D.C. to write their business plan publication...or that we would have the opportunity to work with the 33 incredible women who have so graciously given time to share their stories with you in this book. We are business teachers and consultants...no more...no less. The only thing that has made us stand out among our peers is the power of the pen!

To all of you women entrepreneurs, we have but one thought to share with you. If you like the idea, dare to value your thoughts, dare to write, and dare to let the public judge the worth of your words. Don't be afraid to have the enthusiasm to claim the world as your audience. I think Theodore Roosevelt put the challenge nicely in the words on the next page.

Best wishes to all of our readers. We hope that you have enjoyed reading **The Woman Entrepreneur** as much as we have enjoyed writing it."

Linda & Jerry

"It is not the critic who counts, not the man who points out how the strong man stumbled or where the doer of deeds could have done better.

The credit belongs to the man who is actually in the arena; whose face is marred by dust and sweat and blood; who strives valiantly; who errs and comes short again and again; who knows the great enthusiasms, the great devotions, and spends himself in a worthy cause; who, at the best, knows in the end the triumph of high achievement; and who, at the worst, if he fails, at least fails while daring greatly, so that his place shall never be with those cold and timid souls who know neither victory nor defeat."

Theodore Roosevelt

INFORMATION ON

BOOKS

SOFTWARE

PRESENTATIONS

by

LINDA PINSON
&
JERRY JINNETT

BUSINESS BOOKS & SOFTWARE

by

LINDA PINSON & JERRY JINNETT

1. OUT OF YOUR MIND...AND INTO THE MARKETPLACE⁻

A step-by-step guide for starting and succeeding with a small or home-based business. Takes you through the mechanics of business start-up (business license, DBA's, seller's permit, etc.) and gives an overview of information on such topics as copyrights, trademarks, and patents, legal structures, recordkeeping and marketing.

2. ANATOMY OF A BUSINESS PLAN

Will enable you to research and write your own business plan. Our step-by-step format is designed to take away the mystery and help you to put together a plan that will both satisfy a lender and enable you to analyze your company and implement changes that will insure success.

3. AUTOMATE YOUR BUSINESS PLAN (SOFTWARE)

See the reverse side of this page for software description and order information.

4. MARKETING: RESEARCH & REACH YOUR TARGET MARKET

A comprehensive guide to marketing your business. This book not only shows you how to reach your customers. It also gives you a wealth of information on how to research that market through the use of library resources, questionnaires, demographics, etc.

5. RECORDKEEPING: THE SECRET TO GROWTH & PROFIT

Basic business recordkeeping both explained and illustrated. This book is excellent if you are new to business recordkeeping or if your records are in trouble. It is designed to give a clear understanding of small-business accounting by taking you step-by-step through general records, development of financial statements, tax reporting, the development of a recordkeeping schedule, and financial statement analysis.

6. THE HOME-BASED ENTREPRENEUR

A complete guide to working at home. Topics covered include: history and current status of home business, zoning regulations, tax advantages, marketing, understanding cash flow, pricing/costing your product or service. Extensive reference section for each state.

Our books and software are available in libraries and bookstores or directly from the publisher. Write to: Out of Your Mind...and Into the Marketplace⁻, 13381 White Sand Drive, Tustin, CA 92680 -or- TEL: (714) 544-0248, FAX: (714) 730-1414 (Order Form on page 241)

AUTOMATE YOUR BUSINESS PLAN
FACT SHEET

Technical Requirements:
- IBM PC, AT, or 100% compatible computer
- Hard Drive best, but not required
- 640K of Internal memory
- PCDOS/MSDOS version 2.0 or higher
- Any standard PC compatible printer
- No additional software required

ADDITIONAL BONUSES

1. Within the program, the text editor can also be used as a stand-alone word processor. It incorporates features found in many more expensive word processors including pull down menus and context sensitive help.

2. The spreadsheet can also be used as a stand-alone spreadsheet for simple applications such as budgeting and financial statements. While it doesn't contain all of the features of a full spreadsheet, it is more than adequate for simple calculations.

3. Text and spreadsheets files created within Automate Your Business Plan are in standard ASCII text. That means you can import business plans created using Automate Your Business Plan into documents produced by other word processors such as WordPerfect or Microsoft Word.

ORDER TODAY

Automate Your Business Plan
& Anatomy of a Business Plan
Software & Text Pkg. @ $95.00 _____

CA res. add 7 3/4% sales tax _____

Shipping Fees $4.50 _____

Next Day Air Express $16.00 _____

    TOTAL AMOUNT DUE $_____

Name_____

  Address_____

  City_____

  State_____Zip_____

  Telephone_____

Make Check Payable to: Out of Your Mind...and Into the Marketplace
13381 White Sand Dr., Tustin, CA 92680

Small Business Books
Software

OUT OF YOUR MIND...
AND INTO THE MARKETPLACE™

13381 White Sand Drive, Tustin, CA 92680 (714) 544-0248

PURCHASE ORDER/PRICE LIST

Name/Company _____ Telephone No. _____

Address_____

City_____ State _____ Zip Code _____

Purchase No.: _____Date: _____Ordered By: _____

QUANTITY	TITLE	ISBN NUMBER	PRICE	TOTAL
	A. Automate Your Business Plan (software & textbook)	0-944205-23-2	$95.00	
	B. Anatomy of a Business Plan	0-944205-17-8	$24.00	
	C. Out of Your Mind... and Into the Marketplace™	0-944205-09-9	$22.00	
	D. Marketing: Researching & Reaching Your Target Market	0-944205-12-7	$22.00	
	E. Recordkeeping: The Secret to Growth & Profit	0-944205-14-3	$24.00	
	F. Set of four books (B,C,D,E)	N/A	$85.00	
	G. The Home-Based Entrepreneur	0-944205-13-5	$14.95	
	H. The Woman Entrepreneur	0-944205-18-6	$14.00	

Satisfaction guaranteed or your money back!

Make Check or Money Order Payable to:

**OUT OF YOUR MIND...
AND INTO THE MARKETPLACE™**
13381 White Sand Drive
Tustin, CA 92680
Tel. No. (714) 544-0248

Subtotal	
CA residents add 7¼% sales tax	
TOTAL	
Shipping: $2.50 first book $1.00 each add. book	
TOTAL DUE	

Prices Effective January 1992
Subject to Change Without Notice

241